Ohana Style
Cookbook

Cover Art Work by Rosalie R. Prussing

Designed and Printed by

ISLAND HERITAGE

To Benefit The Hawaii Bone Marrow Donor Registry

Ohana Style

Cookbook

Published by

ISLAND HERITAGE
P U B L I S H I N G

Second Edition, Fourth Printing, 2001

Item No. 24853-000
ISBN-0-89610-370-6

St. Francis Medical Center Licensed

Cover Artwork *Pickled Mango*
©2000 Rosalie R. Prussing

Introduction

'Ohana *in Hawaiian is family; not only parents and their children, but aunts, uncles, cousins, grandparents, neighbors and the community.* 'Ohana *is also a feeling of family that is shared by caring for others.*

This "'Ohana Style Cookbook" started several years ago, when a group of friends got together to help a friend and former classmate, who graduated with them from Hilo High School. This remarkable woman was Patricia Ikeda Tamashiro, who was fighting a battle against leukemia. Pat wanted to share and experience moments with her family and friends like her children's graduations and her daughter's wedding. A marrow transplant and the Hawaii Bone Marrow Donor Registry were her hope for survival. Her friends helped Pat by raising funds to pay for her medical expenses and to assist the Registry.

Pat's courage was admired as she continued raising her family, working and assisting the Registry. Unfortunately, Pat died from complications following her bone marrow transplant. After paying for her medical expenses, the remaining proceeds of the cookbook fund-raiser were donated in her memory to the Hawaii Bone Marrow Donor Registry for the establishment of the Patricia Ikeda Tamashiro Bone Marrow Fund. Through this fund and the sale of this book, others fulfill their dreams of a full life. A portion of the proceeds from this cookbook goes to the Registry to help with the recruiting and testing of potential donors, as well as to educate and increase public awareness.

We would like to thank the following chefs, who allowed us to use their ono *(delicious) recipes in our cookbook: Constantino Areola, formerly with Frantino's Bistro; Sam Choy, from Sam Choy's Restaurant; Glenn Chu from Indigo Restaurant; On Jin Kim, formerly with Hanatei Bistro; Hari Kojima from Hari's Kitchen; Barbara Kono, formerly with Simply Delicious; Steve Neuman from Hawaii Prince Hotel; Sandee Norris, formerly with Crepe Fever and Mocha Java; Russell Siu and Gale Ogawa from 3660 on the Rise; Alan Wong, from Alan Wong's Restaurant; Roy Yamaguchi from Roy's Restaurant.*

For more information about the Hawaii Bone Marrow Donor Registry, St. Francis Medical Center, please call (808) 524-6619.

Measurement Equivalents

3tsp. = 1 Tbsp.

2 Tbsp. = 1 fluid oz.

4 Tbsp. = 1/4 cup

5 Tbsp. + 1 tsp. = 1/3 cup

8 Tbsp. = 1/2 cup
4 fluid oz.

10 Tbsp. + 2 tsp. = 2/3 cup

12 Tbsp. = 3/4 cup

16 Tbsp. = 1 cup
8 fluid oz.

1/4 cup + 2 Tbsp. = 3/8 cup

1/2 cup + 2 Tbsp. = 5/8 cup

3/4 cup + 2Tbsp. = 7/8 cup

2 cups = 16 fluid oz.
1 pint

2 pints = 1 quart

4 quarts = 1 gallon

Table of Contents

Pupus and Dips

Ono Salsa

1	bunch of cilantro	1	4 oz. can Ortega roasted
1/2	can 7-up		jalapeno pepper
1	28 oz. can Six-In-One brand		use: 1/4 can for mild sauce
	ground whole tomato		or 1/2 can for medium/hot
1	28 oz. can S & W premium		sauce or 3/4 can for hot
	ready cut peeled tomato		sauce
1-3	Maui onion (chopped)	2	tsp. garlic salt
1	4 oz. can diced chilies	3	tsp. salt

Use a blender or food processor to mince cilantro leaves with 7-up. Mix all ingredients together in a large bowl, and let sit overnight to blend flavors. Yields approximately 4 1/2 pints. All canned ingredients can be found at Safeway. Will keep for 2 weeks in refrigerator.

Shrimp Dip

1	8 oz. cream cheese	2	4 1/2 oz. cans of shrimp
1/2	cup sour cream		(rinsed and drained)
1/4	cup mayonnaise	1	medium tomato (diced)
1	cup cocktail sauce	2	stalks of green onion(minced)
2	cup mozzarella cheese		

Cream together cream cheese, sour cream and mayonnaise. Spread on 12 inch plate. Spread cocktail sauce over cream cheese layer. Spread mozzarella cheese over cocktail sauce. In a large bowl combine shrimp, tomato and green onions. Sprinkle shrimp mixture over cheese layer and chill. Serve with crackers.

Artichoke Spread

1	10 oz. package frozen artichokes	1	4 oz. can chopped or whole
1	cup mayonnaise		chilies, mild or medium
1	cup parmesan cheese, grated		

Thaw artichokes in microwave oven and chop into bite size pieces. Mix above ingredients. Sprinkle with parmesan cheese and bake for 25 min. in preheated 325 degree oven. Serve with crackers or chips.

Hot Crab Dip

2 cups mayonnaise	1/2 cup grated fresh parmesan cheese
1 8 oz. can artichokes (not marinated)	1/2 cup chopped white or green onion
	1/4 tsp. tabasco sauce
1 cup crab meat or imitation crab meat	1 tsp. parsley flakes
	paprika

Mix all ingredients together and spread in 9" x 9" square or 9" round baking dish. Sprinkle with paprika. Broil 10 minutes before serving or until heated through. Serve with crackers or bread.

Sun-dried Tomato Spread

1 8 oz. light cream cheese
pesto sauce (drain off most of the oil)
sun-dried tomatoes, chopped

Spread block of cream cheese on serving dish. Add a layer of pesto to cover most of the cheese layer. Leave enough cream cheese showing for color. Sprinkle sun-dried tomatoes on top. Serve with crackers.

Smoked Salmon Spread

1 8 oz. cream cheese, softened	dash of tabasco sauce
1/4 cup whipping cream	1 4oz. smoked salmon, gently shredded
1 stalk green onion, thinly sliced	
1 tsp. lemon juice	2 Tbsp. red salmon caviar

Mix cream cheese and whipping cream in a food processor. Add green onion, lemon juice and tabasco. Process until just mixed. Transfer cream cheese mixture to a bowl. Gently fold in smoked salmon and caviar until well combined, but do not overmix. Chill. Serve with bagels, sliced french bread or crackers. Yield: 2 cups.

Spinach Dill Dip

1   box chopped frozen spinach
    (thaw, squeeze out liquid)
1   cup mayonnaise
1   sm. carton plain yogurt or
    sour cream

1/2 cup chopped parsley
1/2 cup chopped green onion
1/2 tsp. dill seed
     salt and pepper to taste
     juice of 1/2 lemon

Mix together. Refrigerate at least five (5) hours. Serve with large tacos or tortilla chips.

Dill Weed and Clam Dip

1   cup mayonnaise
1   8 oz. sour cream
    (do not use imitation)
1   tsp. dill weed spice

1   tsp. Bon Appetit spice
1   tsp. minced or chopped clams
    (drain liquid a little)

Mix all ingredients. Chill until ready to serve.

Crab Mold Dip

1   can cream of mushroom soup
1   8 oz. cream cheese
1   cup mayonnaise
2   stalks celery, minced
5   leaves green onion, minced
1   pkg. unflavored gelatin

2   Tbsp. water
1   can king or snow crab (If
    using canned crab with no
    color, imitation crab strips
    may be added for color)
    dash of tabasco

Heat soup, cream cheese and mayonnaise over low heat until melted. Do not boil, stir constantly. Add celery and onion. Mix together gelatin and water and add to mixture. Add crab and tabasco sauce. Pour into mold and refrigerate.

Serve with crackers or raw vegetables.

Crisp Won Ton

1 lb. ground pork
1/2 can water chestnuts, diced
4 stalks green onions finely sliced
1 pkg. Nice brand long rice (soaked in hot water, drained, and cut into pieces about 1 inch long)

3 eggs
   salt, pepper, ajinomoto to your taste
2 pkgs. won ton pi (about 5 dozen)

Combine pork, water chestnuts, green onions, long rice, eggs, salt, pepper and ajinomoto. Mix well in fairly large mixing bowl.

Fill large pot with about 2 inches of water. Fill empty water chestnut can with water and place in the middle of the pot. Place bowl of pork mixture on can and cover pot. Steam for 20-30 minutes or until pork is cooked. Remove bowl from pot. Drain excess liquid and cool.

Options: 1. Mixture can be eaten after steaming. 2. Wrap in won ton pi and deep fry. 3. Wrap in won ton pi and add to the following soup base:

Boil 2 cans chicken stock and 2 cans water. Add 2 packets dashi, if desired. Add salt and ajinomoto to taste. Garnish with green onions. Left over water chestnuts can be sliced and added to broth.

Won Ton with Crab and Cheese

1 8 oz. cream cheese at room temperature
1/2 tsp. sesame oil
1/4 tsp. steak sauce or shoyu
1/4 tsp. pepper
1 beaten egg
1 1/4 c. thinly sliced garlic chives (flatleaf) – chopped
2 cloves garlic pressed or minced

1/2 lb. imitation crab meat
1 pkg. won ton pi
1 beaten egg (to seal won ton)

Dipping sauce:

1/3 cup red wine vinegar
2 Tbsp. water
1 Tbsp. finely shredded pickled ginger

In a bowl mix all ingredients except won ton pi and beaten egg. Mound 1 tsp. filling in corner of won-ton and fold over to a triangle shape. Moisten edges with beaten egg. Deep fry won-tons until golden brown, about 1 minute. Drain on paper towels and serve with dipping sauce.

Potato Skins

4   trays of frozen potato skins
    Mix in bowl:
1   pkg. Lipton's country style
    vegetable soup
1   cup mayonnaise
1   cup water chestnuts,
    chopped

1   8 oz. sour cream
1   box frozen spinach, thawed
    and chopped (squeeze gently)
    Mix together:
1   pkg. cheddar cheese
1   pkg. mozzarella cheese

Mix ingredients and refrigerate at least two hours (or overnight). Bake frozen skins for 3 to 5 minutes, skin side up. Stuff potatoes, sprinkle with cheddar and mozzarella cheese.

Bake at 350° for 10-15 minutes.

Kilawen

Marinated raw meat appetizer

1   lb. fresh top sirloin steak,
    very lean
    salt or garlic salt
    pepper
1   medium juicy lemon
2   Tbsp. fresh grated ginger

1/4 cup fresh diced green onions
2   tsp. capers, finely chopped
     (optional)
1   medium tomato (optional)
4   Tbsp. shoyu
2   tsp. chili pepper water

Trim off any fat and gristle from steak. Slice steak into 2 1/2" strips, 1/4" thick. Salt and pepper all meat strips to taste. Place meat strips into a quart size bowl and squeeze the juice of the entire lemon onto the meat. Be sure all meat strips are evenly coated with lemon juice. Mix in grated ginger, diced green onions, and chopped capers with the meat strips. Mix well. Halve and slice the tomato into 1/8" slices. Salt and pepper tomato slices to taste. Mix tomato slices in with meat strips. Add shoyu and chili pepper water. Mix well. Garnish with a little more chopped green onions. Serve promptly.

Poisson Cru

A delightful Tahitian way to serve raw fish.

1/2 lb. ahi, ono or mahimahi,
     sliced in bite size pieces
     about 1/4"thick
1/2 cup thinly sliced Maui onion
1/4 cup finely sliced green onion
1/2 cup finely sliced Japan cucumber
1/2 cup tomato, diced
1/2 cup shredded cabbage

1/2 cup coarsely grated carrot
4 Tbsp. fresh coconut milk
     (substitute with frozen or
     canned if fresh is not
     available)
3 Tbsp. fresh lime juice
     salt to taste (optional)

Combine all ingredients in large bowl except for coconut milk, salt and lime juice. Just prior to serving, add coconut milk, salt and then lime juice.

Island Fish Ceviche'

with Avocado, Strawberry Papaya and Chili Peppers
by Roger Dikon - Maui Prince Hotel.

12 oz. boneless filet of blue marlin,
     diced 1/2" square
1 cup freshly squeezed lime juice
1/2 cup freshly squeezed orange juice
2 Tbsp. extra virgin olive oil
3 Tbsp. cilantro, freshly chopped
2 Hawaiian chili peppers.
     freshly chopped

1/2 cup green onions,
     chopped 1/4" lengths
     Hawaiian salt to taste
1/2 large strawberry papaya,
     peeled, seeded and diced
1/2 large firm but ripe avocado,
     peeled, seeded and diced
     lime wheel (for garnish)

Dice the marlin and marinate in the lime juice for 45 minutes. The acidic lime juice will "cook" the fish. It will turn a whitish opaque color. Drain off the excess lime juice that has been absorbed by the fish. Add the orange juice, olive oil, cilantro, chili peppers (to taste), green onions and Hawaiian salt. Mix well and chill until the ceviche' is ice cold. Just before serving, add the diced papaya and avocado and mix gently. Serve in a champagne with a lime wheel garnish.

Poke

2 lbs. fish or tako - chopped	1/2 cup green onion
1/4 cup chopped ogo	1/2 tsp. Hawaiian salt (add
1 clove garlic, chopped	a little more for fish)
1 tsp. sesame seed, crushed	1/2 of a chili pepper
1 Tbsp. oyster sauce	2 tsp. sesame seed oil
1 Tbsp. shoyu	

Combine all ingredients.

Flank Steak Poke

by Roger Dikon - Maui Prince Hotel

16 oz. flank steak, trimmed and peeled	1 Tbsp. Inamona (roasted kukui nut)
1 cup teriyaki sauce	1 Tbsp. roasted dark sesame oil
1 med. Maui onion, cut julienne	1 tsp. patis
1 large vine ripened tomato, diced	1 Tbsp. sambal (chili paste or Hawaiian chili peppers to taste)
1 Tbsp. chopped garlic	1/2 cup green onions, cut into
1 1/2 Tbsp. chopped ginger	1/2" lengths

Marinate the flank steak in the teriyaki sauce for 2 hours. Remove the flank steak and broil over hot coals, preferable Kiawe (Mesquite) charcoal for approximately 4 minutes per side, until it is rare-medium inside.

Slice across the bias and slice again into thin pieces about the size of a quarter. Mix with the remaining ingredients, seasoning to taste with the sambal or chili peppers.

Ahi Katsu with Wasabi - Ginger Butter Sauce

by 3660 on the Rise

8 oz. Ahi	1 oz. water
4 nori sheets	1 cup flour
1 bunch spinach (stemmed & dried)	1 qt. vegetable oil
2 cups panko	salt and black pepper
2 eggs	

Cut ahi into pieces as long as a nori wrapper and 1 inch thick. Spread nori sheets out. Line with spinach. Place one piece of ahi on each sheet. Season with salt and pepper. Top again with spinach. Roll and seal with water. Beat eggs with water and flour. Consistency should be the same as pancake batter. Put flour in one plate and panko in another. Roll wrapped ahi into flour, then into batter mixture and then into the panko breading making sure all parts are covered. Deep fry in hot oil. Turn constantly to allow even browning. Remove and slice.

Wasabi - Ginger Butter Sauce

1 shallot, chopped	1 oz. heavy cream
1 inch ginger, chopped	1 oz. shoyu
1 Tbsp. wasabi	4 oz. unsalted butter
1/4 cup rice vinegar	(cut into 1 oz. cubes)

Put shallot, ginger, wasabi and rice vinegar in a sauce pan on medium high heat and allow vinegar to reduce to about 1 tbsp. Add cream and reduce by one half. Add shoyu and turn heat to low. Whisk in butter cubes one at a time until incorporated. Remove from heat. Place about 1 oz of sauce on plate. Slice ahi rolls into 6 pieces and arrange on wasabi ginger-sauce.

Seared Ahi with Cucumber & Mint Salsa

by Roger Dikon - Maui Prince Hotel

Ahi, sashimi grade (3 oz / 4 each)
blacken spice
cucumber mint salsa
mint leaf
macadamia nut oil

Blacken spice:

2   Tbsp. salt
2   Tbsp. white pepper
2   Tbsp. black pepper
1   Tbsp. thyme
1   Tbsp. dry mustard
1   Tbsp. cayenne
2   Tbsp. garlic salt

Mix ingredients thoroughly.

Salsa:

4   Japanese cucumber, peeled
    and diced small (Brunoise)
    1/2 red onion, diced small
1   red pepper, diced small
1   oz. mint, chopped
1/2 cup rice wine vinegar
1/2 cup Aji mirin
    salt and pepper

Mix ingredients thoroughly.

The Ahi should be in a blocked form for easy slicing. Coat the Ahi with the blacken spices and let it sit for 5 minutes. In a medium saute pan, heat 1 Tbsp. of the macadamia nut oil until just smoking and sear all four sides. Place 1/2 cup salsa on plate. Slice the Ahi, 1/4 inch thick and layer over the salsa. Garnish with a nice sprig of mint.

Seared Ahi on Buckwheat Pasta

with Green Papaya Salad and Oriental Vinaigrette
by Gary Strehl Executive Chef Hawaii Prince Hotel

1   lb. Ahi filet (cut into medallions
    1/2 inch thick)
    salt and pepper
    olive oil
1   med. green papaya (peeled and
    cut julienne)
1   tsp. chili powder
1   tsp. anchovy filet (chopped into
    a paste)
1   tsp. fish sauce (Thailand)
1   med. avocado
1/2 tsp. garlic (minced)
    juices of 2 limes
    juices of 2 lemons
1   lb. dry buckwheat pasta
    (soba noodles) - cooked
    al dente

Salt and pepper ahi and sear quickly in hot skillet with olive oil on all four sides. Place in refrigerator to chill and stop cooking. Combine and mix papayas, chili pepper, anchovy filet, fish sauce, avocado, garlic and juices of limes and lemons to make relish. Place pasta on platter, put daikon sprouts on pasta, spoon relish over sprouts, lay sliced seared ahi on relish with oriental vinaigrette over.

For Oriental Vinaigrette

4   oz. passion juice
8   oz. orange juice
6   oz. shoyu
1   tsp. sesame oil
1   tsp. chili pepper
1   Tbsp. ginger (chopped)
1/2 cup green onions
    (chopped)
2   Tbsp. cilantro (chopped)
1   tsp. sesame seeds (roasted)
1   tsp. ogo (chopped)
    juice of 2 limes

Combine all ingredients and chill overnight.

Charred Ahi

Coated with 7 Japanese Spices in Lilikoi Shoyu Sauce
by On Jin Kim - Hanatei Bistro

3 oz. shichimi (7 Japanese spices)
2 tbsp. olive oil
12 oz. ahi sticks
1/2 piece medium daikon, fine julienne
1/2 piece carrot, fine julienne
1/2 piece Maui onion, finely sliced, marinated in juice from 1/2 of a lemon
1 piece bay leaf
1 piece shallot, sliced

1 cup white wine
6 pieces whole white sliced peppercorns
1/4 cup lilikoi juice, concentrated
1 tbsp. sugar
1 cup cream
1/4 lb. unsalted butter, cut into pieces
1 tbsp. soy sauce

Ahi sticks:

Coat the ahi with shichimi. Heat oil in a fry pan. Add ahi and sear quickly. Slice 3 oz. of ahi per person.

Place daikon, carrot and onion in the middle of a serving plate and arrange sliced ahi and sauce on the front and serve.

Makes 4 servings.

Lilikoi Sauce:

Combine bay leaf, shallot, white wine, peppercorns, likikoi juice and sugar in a sauce pot and reduce until about 2 Tbsp. remains. Add cream and reduce further until about 1/3 remains. Take off the burner. Add all of the butter, piece by piece, mixing constantly with a whip. Add soy sauce to taste.

Seared Ahi or Seared Spencer Steak

with Wasabi Sauce

Ahi steaks or ahi block, sashimi-grade
sesame oil
cilantro, finely chopped
olive oil

Rub ahi with sesame oil then cover with the chopped cilantro. Sear the outside of the ahi in olive oil, making sure the center is raw. Do not over fry. Serve atop the wasabi sauce (recipe follows) and can be garnished with a sprig of cilantro.

Note: The ahi can also be substituted by a spencer steak or rib eye steak. Just follow the directions exactly like you would with the ahi.

Wasabi Sauce

8	Tbsp. plain yogurt	1/2	tsp. Chinese dry mustard paste
6	Tbsp. shoyu	2	tsp. Dijon mustard
1	tsp. wasabi paste		dash of dill

Mix all the ingredients together.

Soups, Salads and Dressings

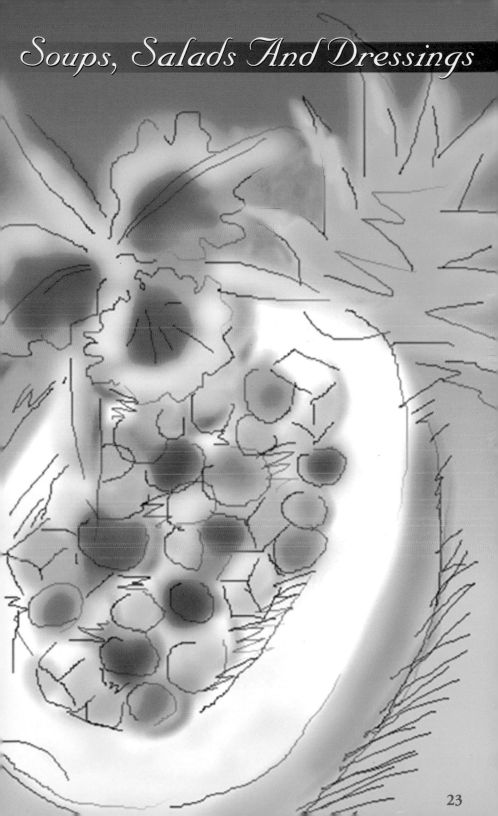

Abalone Soup and Mustard Cabbage

3	dried mushrooms		dash of ajinomoto
2	qts. stock	1	cup carrots (cut into thick
1/2	lb. pork (thinly sliced)		slivers)
1	tsp. ginger juice	1/4	lb. mustard cabbage
1/2	tsp. salt	1	can abalone (cut into strips)

Soak mushrooms in hot water, cut stems and sliver mushrooms. Bring stock to boil. Add mushrooms, pork, ginger juice, seasoning and carrots. Simmer 20 minutes. Cut mustard cabbage. Add cabbage and abalone liquid to soup. Cook uncovered until cabbage is tender. Stir in abalone strips.

Tahitian Crab Meat Soup

by Chef Sam Choy of Sam Choy's Restaurant

2	cups diced onion	2	cups frozen chopped spinach,
1/4	cup butter		thawed or 3 cups chopped
2	Tbsp. flour		fresh spinach, washed and
2	cups heavy cream		steamed
1/2	cup chicken stock	1/2	cup crab meat
2	cups coconut milk		salt and white pepper to taste

In large saucepan, saute onion in butter until translucent. Stir in flour; blend well. Add heavy cream and chicken stock. Simmer for 5 minutes, stirring frequently. Stir in coconut milk, spinach and crab meat. Cook for 3 minutes, stirring frequently. Season to taste with salt and white pepper.

Makes 4 servings.

Imitation Bird's Nest Soup

1	pkg. long rice	5	cups stock
1/2	cup pork	1-1/2	tsp. salt
1/2	cup ham		dash of ajinomoto
1/2	cup dried mushrooms	2	eggs - well beaten
	soaked and sliced	1/2	cup green onions
1	cup bamboo shoots		

Soak long rice in boiling water for 1/2 to 1 hour. Drain and cut into 1" pieces. Chop pork, ham, mushrooms and bamboo shoots 3/4" long. Bring stock to boil and add all ingredients except eggs and onions to stock. Simmer 15-20 minutes. Just before serving stir in eggs and onions.

Supper Soup

2	smoked ham hocks	1/2	cup red wine
2	bay leaves	1	tsp. basil
3	links Italian sausage	1/4	cup chopped parsley
2	onions, chopped	4	red potatoes, cut in chunks
2	cloves garlic, minced	3	stalks celery, sliced
1	28 oz. can tomatoes	2	medium zucchini, sliced
1	8 oz. can tomato sauce	1/2	lb. green beans, ends trimmed, halved

Cook ham hocks in 6 cups water with bay leaves until tender; remove bones. Brown sausage, cut in bite size pieces; reserve oil. Saute onions and garlic; drain oil. Add to ham hocks broth with tomatoes, tomato sauce, wine, seasonings, sausage and vegetables. Simmer 20 to 25 minutes, until vegetables are tender.
Makes 8 to 10 servings.

Scallop Soup

1 can Swanson's chicken broth	Salt to taste
3 cups water	2 bamboo shoots, cut in strips
2 cubes chicken bouillon	4 Tbsp. cornstarch mixed with
1 large dried mushroom, soaked	1/2 cup cold water
and cut in very thin strips	4 eggs
1/4 tsp. sugar	1 can boiled scallops, add
Dash of ajinomoto	liquid with soup stock

Combine chicken broth, water and bouillon cubes in pot. Bring to a boil and add mushroom strips. Simmer for 30 minutes. Add seasoning. Add bamboo shoots and simmer for an additional 10 minutes. Turn heat up and thicken stock with cornstarch mixture. Stir and cool for about two minutes. Beat eggs lightly with chopsticks and add to soup in thin strips, stirring soup with chopsticks so that the egg will cook in thin strips. Turn stove off and add scallops. Thicken slightly if desired.

Mushroom Barley Soup

3 cups mushroom slices	2 cups milk
(about 1/2 lb.)	1/2 cup quick barley
1/2 cup chopped round onion	2 tsp. Worcestershire sauce
1/2 cup chopped green pepper	1 1/2 tsp. salt
1/3 cup butter or margarine	1 tsp. dried parsley flakes
1/3 cup flour	dash of pepper
3 cups water	

Saute mushrooms, onion and green pepper in butter. Blend in flour; continue cooking over medium heat until flour is browned. Gradually add water and milk; add remaining ingredients. Bring to boil, stirring frequently; reduce heat. Cover and simmer 10 to 20 minutes or until barley is tender, stirring occasionally. Makes 6 to 8 servings.

Portuguese Bean Soup

"3660 On the Rise"

6 oz. dry red kidney beans (soak over night in water)	1 tsp. paprika
1 Tbsp. oil	1/8 tsp. marjoram
2 6 oz. stick Portuguese sausage	1/8 tsp. basil
1/2 cup carrots, diced large	2 qts. beef or chicken stock
1 cup onions, diced large	1 smoked ham hock
3/4 cup celery, diced large	1 cup potato, diced
1/2 cup bell pepper, diced large	2 cups cabbage, diced large
1 Tbsp. garlic, chopped	1 can diced tomato or 2 cups fresh tomatoes
1 tsp. ginger, chopped	salt and pepper to taste
1 each bay leaf	

Clean and soak beans overnight. In a large pot with low flame, heat oil. Saute the sausage until fat is rendered. Increase heat and add the diced vegetables (except cabbage and tomato) and saute till transparent (around 5 minutes). Add garlic, ginger and herbs.

Stir and saute for about 2 minutes. Add stock and ham hock and simmer for about an hour. Add beans and potatoes about half hour after stock boils. When beans are soft add cabbage and tomatoes and continue to cook. Remove the ham hock and dice. Return to soup and season with salt and pepper. Thicken slightly if desired.

Corn Chowder

1/2 lb. bacon, diced	4 cups milk
1 onion, chopped (about 1/2 cup)	2 large cans cream-style corn
1/2 cup celery, chopped	1-2 potatoes, cooked and diced
2 Tbsp. flour	salt, pepper

In large skillet, fry bacon until crisp. Remove and drain, save 3 Tbsp. drippings. Add onion and celery to drippings, cook and stir until onion is tender. Remove from heat, blend in flour. Cook over low heat, stirring until bubbly. Remove from heat. Stir in milk and bring to almost a boil, stirring constantly. Stir in corn and potatoes. Add salt and pepper to taste. Stir in bacon just before serving.

Vegetable-burger Soup

1/2	lb. ground beef	1	10-oz. pkg. frozen mixed
1	1-lb. can stewed tomatoes		vegetable
1	8-oz. can tomato sauce	1/2	envelope (1/4 cup) dry onion
2	cups water		soup mix
		1	tsp. sugar

In large heavy saucepan, lightly brown ground beef. Drain off excess fat. Stir in tomatoes, tomato sauce, water, frozen vegetables, onion soup mix and sugar. Bring to boil. Reduce heat, cover and simmer 20 minutes. Makes 6 to 8 servings.

Black Bean Soup

1/2	large onion, chopped	1	tsp. cumin
3	garlic cloves, chopped	1	tsp. coriander
	olive oil	1	tsp. oregano
2	15-oz.. cans black beans,	2	bay leaves
	(1 can will be drained, the	1/2	tsp. thyme
	other left in it's own juices...	1/2	cup tomato paste
	Progresso brand is best, but	1	bunch fresh cilantro, chopped
	if unavailable, that's okay.)		
1	can chicken broth		

Saute the onion and garlic in a little olive oil. Remove from heat, and add 1 can of the black beans, undrained. Pour this into a blender and quickly puree. Return to sauce pan and heat. Add the remaining can of drained beans, chicken broth, all the spices, and the tomato paste. Simmer on low for about 10 to 15 minutes... then add the chopped cilantro. Serve. You can garnish this with more fresh cilantro and for those who like 'hot' food, you can garnish this with jalapeno peppers.

Minestrone Soup

3-4 slices bacon
2 cloves garlic, mashed
1 cup chopped onions
1 lb. hamburger
1 can Campbell's Beef Broth
1 can Campbell's Bean and
    Bacon

1 1/2 can water
1 16 oz. can stewed tomatoes
1/2 tsp. salt
1 tsp. basil leaves
1 cup shell macaroni
1/2 cup chopped celery
1 cup zucchini

Chop bacon and brown. Add mashed garlic, stir until slightly brown. Add onions and cook until transparent. Add hamburger, cook until done and drain some of fat. Add broth, bean & bacon soup, water and stewed tomatoes. Bring to boil. Add salt, basil leaves and macaroni. Simmer for 1/2 hour. Add celery and zucchini last.

Caesar Style Salad

1 head romaine lettuce
   juice of 1 lemon
1/2 teaspoon salt
   Dash black pepper
2 whole eggs
1 heaping teaspoon Dijon mustard
2 cloves garlic finely chopped

3 tsp. anchovies (finely
   chopped or paste)
1/8 cup red wine vinegar
1 1/4 cup olive oil
1/2 cup parmesan cheese
   Dash Worcestershire sauce
   Pinch of sugar

Rinse lettuce and dry. Refrigerate wrapped in paper towels for several hours.

Whisk lemon juice, salt, pepper, eggs, mustard, garlic and anchovies together. Slowly whisk in vinegar. Add oil in a steady stream as you continue to whisk ingredients. Add parmesan cheese, worcestershire sauce and sugar.

Toss lettuce thoroughly with 1/2 cup of dressing. Garnish with croutons, hard cooked eggs or freshly grated parmesan cheese if desired.

Refrigerated dressing will keep for 2 weeks.

Chinese Chicken Salad

with Hoi Sin Dressing and Chicken Marinade
by "3660 On the Rise"

1/2	red onion sliced thin		lettuce
1	cup rice vinegar	1	carrot shredded
2	boneless chicken breast	1/2	bunch green onions julienne
1/2	lb. mesclun mix	8	won ton pi julienne and fried
1	pkg. soba noodles - cooked	1	Tbsp. black sesame seeds

Soak sliced red onions in rice vinegar for 1/2 hour. Grill marinated chicken breasts and set aside. Toss mesclun mix with about 1/2 cup dressing. Divide onto 6 plates. Toss soba noodles with dressing and divide into 6 equal parts. Place noodles on lettuce. Place marinated onions on soba noodles. Top with shredded carrots and julienne green onion. Slice chicken breast and divide into six portions. Arrange chicken around salad. Sprinkle fried won ton pi around the perimeter of the plate. Garnish with black sesame seeds.

Hoi Sin Dressing:

1/2	cup hoi sin sauce	1/4	cup sesame oil
1/2	cup lemon juice	1/4	cup rice vinegar
3/4	cup salad oil	3	Tbsp. sugar

Mix all ingredients together till emulsified.

Chicken Marinade:

1/2	cup Lime juice	1/4	cup soy sauce
3	Tbsp. garlic		pinch crushed red chilies
2	inches ginger grated	1	cup vegetable oil

Combine all ingredients and mix till emulsified. Marinate chicken breast for at least one day in refrigerator. Remove and grill when needed.

Chinese Vegetable Salad I

1   small pkg. won ton pi chips
1   med. head romaine lettuce,
      sliced or broken into pieces
1   small head iceberg lettuce,
      sliced or broken into pieces
1/4   cup Chinese parsley
1/2   cup green onions, chopped

1/2   lb. char siu, slivered
1   cup cooked chicken, sliced
      (Hulihuli, roasted or broiled
      chicken)
Optional:
      Sliced cucumber
      Sliced water chestnuts

Wash vegetables, drain thoroughly. Tear greens into bite size pieces. Add parsley and green onions. Chill well. Before serving, add won ton chips and top with char siu and chicken. Toss with Chinese sesame dressing.

Chinese Sesame Dressing

3   Tbsp. sesame oil
3   Tbsp. vegetable oil
4   Tbsp. vinegar

1/2   tsp. salt
2   tsp. sugar
      Black pepper
      Toasted sesame seeds

Combine ingredients in pint jar and shake well. Pour dressing over vegetable salad just before serving.

Note. Use Japanese vinegar for milder dressing.

Chinese Vegetable Salad II

Salad:

Manoa lettuce
Iceberg lettuce
Chinese parsley
Green onion
Water chestnuts

Char siu
Chicken, shredded
Sesame seeds, sprinkle over
Won ton chips

Dressing:

3/4　cup hoi sin sauce
1-1/8　cup sesame seed oil
3/4　cup white vinegar
2　tsp. salt

1-1/2　cups ketchup
1-1/8　cups salad oil
1-1/2　cups sugar
2　tsp. ajinomoto

Blend together dressing ingredients. Layer salad ingredients in order. Before serving, pour amount of dressing needed and toss.

Spinach Salad

2　10-oz. fresh spinach (horenso)
6　hard boiled eggs (chopped)
1　lb. bacon fried and crumbled

Dressing:

1　cup salad oil
5　Tbsp. red wine vinegar
4　Tbsp. sour cream
1 1/2　tsp. salt
1/2　Tbsp. dry mustard

2　Tbsp. sugar
2　tsp. chopped parsley
2　cloves garlic, crushed
coarsely ground black pepper

Mix dressing 24 hours before serving. Toss spinach with dressing. Garnish with chopped egg and bacon.

To keep salad crisp, put chopped egg and bacon in separate containers and let everyone prepare their own salad.

Warm Spinach Salad

by "3660 On the Rise"

1   bunch spinach, destemmed
1   cup warm pancetta-tarragon
    vinaigrette
1   cup sliced mushrooms

1   cup 1/4 cut artichoke hearts
1   cup diced tomatoes
1/2 cup chopped hard cooked egg

Place spinach in a large bowl and set aside. In a large saute pan, heat the vinaigrette. Add mushrooms, artichoke hearts and tomato and stir gently. Pour the warm mixture over the spinach. With tongs, toss the spinach with vinaigrette. Place on plate and garnish with chopped egg.

Pancetta-Tarragon Vinaigrette

1/4 cup diced pancetta (or bacon)
1/4 cup onion, diced fine
1   Tbsp. chopped garlic
    red wine vinegar
1/2 tsp. chopped basil
    (or pinch of dried)

1/4 tsp. chopped tarragon
    (or pinch of dried)
1   Tbsp. Dijon mustard
3/4 cup olive oil
1   Tbsp. honey
    salt and pepper to taste

In a small sauce pan, render bacon over medium heat until half way cooked. Add onion and garlic and continue to saute until translucent. Deglaze with red wine vinegar and add herbs. Let steep a few minutes. Add mustard and oil, and season with honey, salt and pepper.

Cabbage Salad

1 medium head cabbage
green onions
sesame seeds

1 can chow mein noodles
shredded cooked chicken
(optional)

Dressing:

1 1/2 tsp. salt
3/4 tsp. pepper
little less than 1/2 cup
vegetable oil

4 1/2 Tbsp. vinegar
3 Tbsp. sugar

Cut cabbage fine like for cole slaw and rinse well. Shake off excess water. Wash and dice green onions. Put dressing ingredients in a jar and shake well. Spread cabbage in a bowl. Top with green onions, sesame seeds, chow mein noodles and dressing.

Won Bok Salad

1-2 heads won bok cabbage, sliced very thin
celery, sliced thin
shredded cooked chicken, optional
1 pkg. won ton pi chips

Dressing:

1 cup vegetable oil or 1/2 cup
sesame oil
1/2 cup sugar
1/2 cup vinegar
1/4 cup mayonnaise
2 tsp. salt

1 tsp. dry mustard
1 clove garlic, minced
1/2 tsp. pepper
1 medium onion, diced
1/4 cup toasted sesame seeds

Mix dressing ingredients together in a blender and blend till dressing is smooth and creamy. Refrigerate until time to serve salad. Toss dressing together with salad ingredients above.

3 Week Slaw

1	large head cabbage, shredded	1	small jar pimento olives, sliced
1	medium onion, chopped	1	cup sugar
1	green pepper, chopped		

Mix cabbage, onion, pepper and olives.   Sprinkle 1 cup sugar over vegetables and let stand.

Bring to a boil the following ingredients and pour over cabbage while hot:

1	Tbsp. sugar	1	tsp. celery seed
1	Tbsp. salt	1	cup cider vinegar
1	tsp. dry mustard	3/4	cup salad oil

Cover tightly and refrigerate overnight. Keeps for 3 weeks.

Coriander Chicken Salad

3	chicken breasts, poached	1	green onion, minced
1/4	cup sesame oil	2	oz. vermicelli or bean thread,
1/4	cup white vinegar		broken into 3" pieces
2	Tbsp. soy sauce	1	head of lettuce, shredded
2-3	Tbsp. sugar	2	bunches green onions, slivered
1	tsp. crushed red pepper	1	bunch cilantro, chopped
3	cloves garlic, minced	1	Tbsp. sesame seeds, toasted

Shred chicken. Mix next 7 ingredients together for dressing. Deep fry the rice vermicelli or bean thread. This will puff up very quickly in hot oil. Drain on paper towels. 10 minutes before serving, mix the shredded head lettuce, slivered green onions, cilantro, sesame seeds, crispy rice vermicelli, chicken and dressing together. Toss well and serve.

Make 6 - 8 servings

Note: The rice vermicelli or bean thread purchased at Thai grocery stores is best.

Chicken Cucumber Salad

2   cucumbers (cut in long cubes)
12 chicken thighs

Directions:
Soak cucumbers in ice water. Boil chicken in salt water for 20 minutes. Debone and chop into pieces.

Dressings:

5   tsp. sugar
1/2 cup vinegar
1/2 cup shoyu
2-3 stalks green onions (chopped)
2   Tbsp. roasted white
     sesame seeds

2   cloves of garlic (chopped)
1-2 red chili peppers (chopped)
1   tsp. ajinomoto
    Chinese parsley to garnish

Place cut cucumbers in a bowl, and add chicken and parsley. Mix dressing ingredients together and add sauce to salad before serving.

Chicken Fajita Salad

1/2 cup mayonnaise, low calorie
     or no cholesterol type
1/2 cup chunky salsa
1   lb. boneless chicken breasts
1   red pepper, quartered
1   yellow pepper, quartered

1   zucchini, sliced
1   onion, cut into wedges and
     skewered
    oil
    Lettuce leaves
    Flour tortillas (optional)

For Salsa dressing:

Combine mayonnaise and salsa. Cover and chill.

Brush chicken, peppers, zucchini and onion with oil. Grill or broil until chicken is done and vegetables are tender. To serve, cut chicken and peppers into strips; arrange with zucchini and onion on lettuce-lined plates. Serve with dressing over top and flour tortillas if desired. Serves 2 as a main entree.

Three Bean Salad

1   can garbanzo beans, drained
1   can kidney beans, drained
1   can green beans, drained
1/2 onion, diced
1/2 bell pepper, diced
     salt & pepper to taste

Dressing:

3/4 cup sugar
1/2 cup vinegar
1/4 cup oil

Mix sauce in separate bowl. Combine remaining ingredients and add sauce. Marinate overnight.

Lehua Salad

2   bunches spinach, washed,
     trimmed and torn into
     bite size pieces
1   tsp. sugar, divided
6   hard cooked eggs, chopped
1/2 lb. ham, julienned
1   pkg. petite frozen peas,
     partially thawed

1   round onion, thinly sliced
     and separated into rings
1   cup sour cream
1   cup mayonnaise
     Curry powder (optional)
1/2 lb. Swiss cheese, grated
1   lb. bacon, cooked, drained
     and crumbled

Arrange half of spinach on bottom of 4 qt. shallow glass serving bowl. Sprinkle with 1/2 tsp. sugar. Place eggs in layer on spinach. Layer ham on eggs. Top with remaining spinach and sprinkle with remaining sugar. Spread peas on spinach; arrange onion on peas.

Combine sour cream and mayonnaise, seasoning with curry if desired. Spread evenly on salad and to edges to seal. Chill covered overnight. When ready to serve, sprinkle with cheese and bacon.

Rice Salad

4 cup cooked rice	1/2 cup chopped black olives,
Canned sweet red peppers,	(Kalamata or other
rinsed and diced	brine olives)
1/2 cup golden raisins	1/4 cup fresh parsley
1 10-oz. pkg frozen peas	1/2 cup chopped fresh dill
	salt and pepper

Combine all ingredients. Add vinaigrette and leave overnight in refrigerator for flavors to blend.

Vinaigrette:

2 Tbsp. Dijon mustard	3/4 cup olive oil
1/4 cup vinegar	sugar to taste

Mix all ingredients.
Serves 8. Goes well with barbecued chicken.

Rice, Olive & Caper Salad

1/4 cup olive oil	1/2 red onion, diced
1/4 cup balsamic vinegar or red	1/2 cup sliced pitted black
wine vinegar	olives (preferably
1/2 tsp. Dijon mustard	Kalamata)
2 clove garlic, minced	1/2 cup sliced green olives
2 cup cooked brown or white	1/4 cup capers, drained
rice, room temperature	1/4 cup pine nuts, toasted
1 large tomato, seeded, diced	

Whisk oil, vinegar, mustard and garlic to blend in a small bowl (or combine all ingredients in a bottle and shake).

Combine remaining ingredients in a medium bowl. Pour dressing over and toss to blend. Season with salt and pepper, if desired.

Can be prepared 2 hours ahead. Let stand at room temperature. Stir well before serving.

Makes 6 - 8 servings.

Tabouli Salad

Salad:

1   cup bulgur (cracked fine or medium)
2   cups boiling water
2   ripe tomatoes - seeded and diced small

1/4   cup finely chopped green onion
1   cup finely chopped parsley
3   Tbsp. chopped fresh mint
6   oz. cream cheese - optional

Dressing:

1/4   cup lemon juice
2   Tbsp. olive oil
1/2   tsp. salt, if desired

1/4   tsp. black pepper
1/4   cup balsamic vinegar
1/4   cup sugar

In a medium bowl, soak the bulgur in the boiling water for 1 hour. Drain bulgur well, pressing out excess water through a fine strainer or cloth. Add tomato, green onions, parsley and mint to bulgur, combine well. Mix all dressing ingredients in a small bowl and add to bulgur mixture and toss the salad to coat ingredients thoroughly. Serve chilled as a salad or, as an option, place cream cheese on a large serving platter. Spoon bulgur salad mixture covering the cream cheese. Serve with crackers as spread.

Linguine Salad

1   pkg. linguine
1/2   bottle Tropics Oriental Salad Dressing
1   pkg. imitation crab meat, shredded
2   cucumbers, cut julienne style
10   oz. taegu, cut into bite sized pieces
1/3   bottle Furikake nori

Boil linguine according to instructions. Cool, then mix everything together.

Soba Salad

1/3 pkg. hijiki	1 pkg. 4 oz. daikon sprouts
1 Tbsp. salad oil	1/2 Maui onion, sliced thin
1 Tbsp. sugar	1 bunch watercress
1 Tbsp. soy sauce	1 small Japanese cucumber, julienned
1 pkg. 0.25 oz. wakame	1 small carrot, sliced thin
2 pkg. 8 oz. soba noodles	

Soak hijiki in warm water for about 20 minutes. Rinse and drain. In small skillet, pan fry hijiki with oil, then add sugar and soy sauce. Cook until liquid is absorbed. Soak wakame for 15 minutes and chop. Set aside.

Dressing:

3/4 cup soy sauce	3/4 cup salad oil
3/4 cup sugar	6 Tbsp. lemon juice
4 Tbsp. Japanese vinegar	

Mix ingredients together. Add 6 Tbsp. of dressing to sliced onions, carrots and wakame. Let stand awhile.

Cook soba noodles as directed on package. Rinse. Cut off ends of daikon and watercress. Layer ingredients on a large platter in this order: soba, wakame mixture, cucumber, watercress, hijiki and daikon sprouts. Serve with additional dressing.

Hot Potato Salad

2 cups boiled salad potatoes, diced	1/2 tsp. salt
1 can shrimp (drained)	1 cup diced celery
1 can crab meat (drained)	1 cup diced round onion
1 cup mayonnaise	chopped parsley

Mix all ingredients and bake at 450 degrees for 10 minutes. Place under broiler for a few minutes to brown top, if desired.

Deluxe Tuna Salad

1 6-1/8 oz. can chunk light tuna, drained and flaked	1/2 cup cheese, diced (Monterey Jack, Swiss or Cheddar)
1/2 cup celery, diced	2 Tbsp. sweet pickle relish
1/2 cup carrot, diced	1/2 cup mayonnaise
1/2 cup raisins	2 tsp. dijon mustard
1/2 cup walnut, chopped	1/4 tsp. curry powder
1/4 cup green onion, chopped	salt to taste

Mix all ingredients together. Add more mayonnaise if desired. Cover and chill 1 to 2 hours. Good on crackers or as a sandwich spread.

French Dressing

1 can tomato soup	2 Tbsp. worcestershire sauce
3/4 cup vinegar	2 cloves garlic
2 tsp. salt	4 tsp. onions (chopped fine)
1/2 tsp. paprika	1 1/2 cup sugar
1 tsp. black pepper	1/4 cup Wesson oil

Blend all ingredients well in blender.

Luxembourg Dressing

4 cloves garlic, finely minced	1 1/2 Tbsp. mixed salad herbs
1/3 cup balsamic vinegar	1 cup olive oil
2 Tbsp. fresh lemon juice	salt and pepper to taste
1 1/2 Tbsp. Dijon mustard	

Whisk garlic, vinegar, lemon juice and mustard together. Whisk in the herbs. Gradually whisk in the oil. Season to taste with salt and pepper.

Salad Dressing

1/2	cup mayonnaise	1/2	tsp. pepper
1	tsp. dry Coleman mustard	3/4	cup sugar
1	cup oil	2	tsp. salt
1/2	cup Japanese Vinegar	1	clove garlic, grated

Blend mayonnaise until smooth, add dry mustard and other ingredients to blender or hand mixer. Refrigerate in jar.

Steak Sauce

1	block butter (1/4 lb.)	3	Tbsp. shoyu
	or margarine	1	tsp. Coleman mustard
4	Tbsp. ketchup	2	tsp. lemon juice

Melt butter on stove and add remaining ingredients. Good with steak, salmon, pork chops and chicken.

Sweet - Sour Sauce

7	Tbsp. sugar	1	Tbsp. oil
3	Tbsp. shoyu		cornstarch and water,
4	Tbsp. vinegar		to thicken

Cook sugar, shoyu, vinegar and oil on range until it boils. Thicken with cornstarch and water mixture. Serve with lumpia or fried chicken.

Basic Sushi Mixture

1	cup Japanese vinegar	1	Tbsp. salt
1	cup sugar	2	tsp. ajinomoto

Cook 5 rice cooker cups rice (3 3/4 standard cups). Mix ingredients together. Use mixture in rice according to your own taste. Vinegar mixture can also be used for namasu.

For about 10 rolls of makizushi.

Shabu Shabu Sauce

4	Tbsp. white sesame seed	1	Tbsp. sake or mirin
2	Tbsp. sugar	3	Tbsp. rice vinegar
2	Tbsp. shoyu	1/2	Tbsp. sesame oil or
1	Tbsp. white wine		hot chili oil

Mix all ingredients well.

Li Hing Mui Pickled Mango

2	cups cider vinegar	1/2	tsp. Chinese five spice
5	cups brown sugar	1	large pkg. seedless li hing mui
1/2	cup Hawaiian salt		Mango slices, chopped
6	cups water		

Boil ingredients except li hing mui and mango slices. Cool and add li hing mui. Pour over bottled mango slices. Store in refrigerator. Ready to eat in 3 days.

Note: Enough liquid for 2 gallons. Any kind of mango can be used.

Cucumber Namasu

4-5 Japan cucumbers   1/4 cup vinegar
1/2 cup sugar   1 Tbsp. Hawaiian salt

Slice cucumbers. Boil sugar, vinegar and salt until sugar dissolves.
Remove from heat. Pour hot mixture over cucumbers. Cool and refrigerate.
Note: If sauce is boiled too long, it will thicken.

Pickled Cucumbers

6-8 cucumbers   1/8 cup Hawaiian salt
  2 cups water   3 chili peppers, chopped
  1 cup sugar   (optional)

Boil water, sugar and Hawaiian salt until sugar dissolves. Cool completely.
Score cucumber skins with a fork. Cut into wedges. Add cucumbers and chili
peppers to sauce in a large jar. Let sit two days minimum in refrigerator.

Mustard Cucumber Koko

  3 Japanese cucumbers
  3 Tbsp. Hawaiian salt
     Sauce:
  1 cup sugar
  1 cup shoyu
1/2 cup vinegar
  4 tsp. mustard (powder)

Slice cucumbers and sprinkle salt over cucumbers. Wait three hours,
then add sauce. (Do not cook sauce.)

Li Hing Cucumber

6-7	Japanese cucumbers, sliced	2	Tbsp. salt
1/2	cup sugar	1	pkg. li hing mui (6 to 7 seeds)

Combine all ingredients and soak overnight. Do not drain.

Bread and Butter Pickles

5	medium cucumbers, sliced	2	clove garlic, minced
1-1/2	lb. Maui onions, sliced thin	1/3	cup Hawaiian salt
		2-3	cups ice cubes

Pickling Mixture:

1/2	tsp. mustard seed	4	cups sugar
1/2	tsp. celery seed	1/2	tsp. grated ginger
2	cups white vinegar		

Place cucumbers, onions and garlic in large bowl. Sprinkle with Hawaiian salt and soak with ice cubes for 30 minutes. Combine mustard seed, celery seed, vinegar, sugar and grated ginger in a pot. Bring to a boil and cook until sugar is dissolved. Cool. Squeeze out water from vegetables and place in a large jar. Pour cooled pickling mixture over vegetables and refrigerate.

Cabbage Tsukemono

1-1/2 cup water
1/4 cup vinegar
1 Tbsp. sake
1 Tbsp. sugar

1/4 cup Hawaiian salt
head cabbage or Chinese
cabbage - chopped

Boil water, vinegar and sake with sugar and salt until they are dissolved. While hot, pour on washed head cabbage or Chinese cabbage.

Seasoned Salt

5 lb. Hawaiian salt
1/3 cup coarse black pepper
5 Tbsp. chopped garlic

5 Tbsp. grated ginger
Crushed chili pepper to taste
(optional)

Mix salt and pepper in large roasting pan. Add garlic and ginger using back of a large wooden spoon to smash and mix in well. Bake at 350 degrees for about 20-30 minutes, or until brown and dry. Stir every 3-5 minutes. Cool and store in bottles.

Great on steaks, fish and chicken on the hibachi. Add a pinch of seasoned salt to soups or stews.

Notes

Pastas & Vegetables

Pastas and Vegetables

Corned Beef Noodle Casserole

1   pkg. (12 oz) wide noodles,
    prepared as directed
    on package
1   can (12 oz) corned beef,
    break into small chunks
1   can cream of chicken soup
1   soup can water or milk

1   small onion, chopped or
    sliced thin
1   small green bell pepper,
    chopped or sliced thin
    cheese of your choice,
    any amount, grated

Combine all ingredients and mix lightly being careful not to break the noodles. Place in a large greased casserole dish. Spread cheese on top, cover and bake at 350 degrees for 25 to 30 minutes.

Optional: Add 1 cup frozen mixed vegetables.

Pasta with Fresh Tomatoes, Basil, Garlic and Roasted Yellow Peppers

10 fresh roma tomatoes
1   bunch basil
3-5 cloves garlic to taste
3   Tbsp. balsamic vinegar
2   Tbsp extra virgin olive oil

    fresh ground pepper
    fresh oregano
1   yellow sweet pepper
    penne or angel hair pasta
    fresh basil leaf

Dice tomatoes, mince basil, mince garlic and mix everything together with the vinegar and oil. Add some fresh ground pepper. Set aside to marinate. Fresh oregano would also be good to add at this point. Roast yellow pepper under the broiler by cutting it in half and putting it under the broiler skin side up on a cookie sheet for about 10 to 15 minutes or until skin is black. Put pepper in a plastic bag to sweat for about 5 minutes. Skin will peel right off. Dice pepper and set aside. Prepare 1 package of pasta. Penne or angel hair would be great. Just before serving heat tomato mixture over medium heat until heated adding diced pepper. Mix heated sauce with cooked pasta. Garnish with fresh basil leaf.

Pasta with Clam Sauce

pasta
1 onion, minced
1/2 cup butter
5 cloves fresh garlic, minced
2 Tbsp. fresh oregano, chopped
1 Tbsp. fresh basil, chopped
1 Tbsp. fresh thyme, chopped
3 cans clams, chopped–save juice

1/2 cup flour
1 cup white wine
12 oz. clam juice
1 1/2 qt. whipping cream
salt and pepper to taste

Cooked pasta of your choice. Saute onion in 1/4 cup of butter until clear. Add garlic (do not burn). Add oregano, basil, thyme and clams. Add balance of butter. Add flour and stir until evenly distributed; using wooden spoon. Add white wine and clam juice. Simmer awhile (reduce by 1/2). Add cream. Simmer until it thickens. Season with salt and pepper to taste. Pour over cooked pasta.

Clam Linguine

1 chopped bell pepper
1 chopped onion
1 tray sliced fresh mushrooms

3 cloves chopped garlic
1 block butter
4-6 Tbsp. flour

Saute all of the above ingredients in 1 block of butter except flour for 5 minutes. Then stir in flour.

2 cans minced clams
2 cans chopped clams
1 pt. half & half
2 Tbsp. sherry
1/2 tsp. pepper

1/2 tsp. thyme
1/2 tsp. sugar
1/2 tsp. salt
2 Tbsp. chopped parsley
1/2 cup parmesan cheese

Add liquid from 2 cans minced clams and 2 cans chopped clams slowly to sauteed bell pepper and onion mixture. Add 1 pt. half & half. Stir until slightly thickened. Add the rest of the above ingredients, except clams. Add clams just before serving.

Fresh Eggplant Fettucine

with Fresh Roma Tomato Sauce

by Chef Constantino Areola from Frantino's Bistro

1 lb. Italian plum tomatoes	spinach fettucine, cooked
1 medium onion	shredded mozzarella
5 garlic cloves, peeled and minced	roasted Japanese eggplant,
1-2 Tbsp. extra virgin olive oil	sliced lengthwise
fresh basil	red bell pepper,
oregano	roasted and cut in strips
salt, and pepper	

Cut tomatoes and onions in large cubes. Toss with garlic and 1-2 tablespoons olive oil in a roasting pan. Roast in a 350° oven for approximately 30 minutes or until lightly roasted. Puree in blender to desired texture (preferably chunky) with fresh basil, oregano, salt and pepper to taste. Simmer in pot until thickened over medium heat (approximately 25 minutes). Place cooked spinach fettucine on an oven safe plate, top with sauce, shredded mozzarella, roasted eggplant and strips of red bell pepper. Place under broiler until cheese has melted.

Chris's Pasta

1/2 lb. mild Italian sausage	1 8 oz. can tomato sauce
2 cups water	1/2 cup frozen cut leaf spinach
1 can Great Northern Beans, drained	1 tsp. Italian seasoning
1 14 1/2 oz. can Italian style stewed tomatoes, undrained, cut up	2 cups uncooked wagon wheel pasta
	parmesan cheese, grated

Brown sausage in large saucepan, drain. Add water, beans, tomatoes, tomato sauce, spinach and seasoning; bring to boil. Stir in pasta. Return to boil. Reduce heat; simmer uncovered 20 to 25 minutes or until pasta is done. Stir occasionally. Serve with grated parmesan cheese. (Spicy sausage can be used for tangier flavor.)

Spaghettini with Scallops and Olive Oil Sauce

1	lb. fresh bay or sea scallops	1	Tbsp. very finely chopped garlic
	salt to taste	1/2	cup olive oil
1	lb. spaghettini or angel hair pasta	2	Tbsp. finely chopped cilantro
1/2	cup unseasoned dry bread crumbs		crushed red pepper

Rinse the scallops in cold water and pat thoroughly dry with a cloth towel. If using sea scallops, cut into 3/8 inch pieces.

Bring a large pot of water to a boil. Add little salt and cook pasta until al dente. Drain well.

Meanwhile, in a small skillet, stir the bread crumbs over high heat until lightly toasted. Transfer to a plate to cool.

In a large saucepan, cook the garlic in the olive oil over moderate heat until it becomes light gold. Add the cilantro and crushed red pepper to taste and stir twice, then add the scallops and one or two large pinches of salt, if desired. Cook over high heat, stirring frequently, until the scallops lose their shine and turn a flat white. Do not overcook the scallops or they will become tough.

Toss the scallop mixture with the pasta. Add the bread crumbs, toss again and serve at once.

Makes 4 to 6 servings.

Note: Do not confuse spaghettini with spaghetti. Spaghettini is thinner. Angel hair pasta also works very well.

Korean Somen with Zucchini

1/2	pound somen noodles, or other type of thin noodles
3	Tbsp. butter or margarine
1	large zucchini (or 2 small ones), cut into 1/4 inch slices, then julienned into 1/8 inch strips

1/2	large onion, sliced
	salt and pepper to taste
1	tbsp. garlic powder
	red pepper flakes to taste
	dash of MSG
	dash of vinegar
1/2	cup soy sauce
2	Tbsp. sesame oil

Topping:

kamaboku
nori
eggs – fried, julienned

Boil somen 10 to 12 minutes. Drain noodles. Refrigerate while preparing the zucchini in its sauce.

For the sauce, heat skillet on medium heat. Melt butter; add julienned zucchini and sliced onion and stir. Add salt, pepper, garlic powder, red pepper flakes, MSG and vinegar. Continue to stir until the zucchini is almost cooked. Add soy sauce and sesame oil.

Add cold noodles to the zucchini and sauce in the skillet. Thoroughly mix. Place in large bowl, cover with plastic wrap and refrigerate at least 30 minutes. Serve cold.

You can top noodles with kamaboku slices, nori (drained seaweed) and fried eggs sliced julienne-style.

Tortellini with Bleu Cheese

1/2 cup half and half cream
  2 stalks green onion, sliced thin

3 oz. bleu or stilton cheese
1 lb. cheese tortellini, cooked

Heat cream with green onion. Crumble in bleu or stilton cheese. Toss with cooked cheese tortellini and serve.

Butter, Cheese and Garlic Pasta Sauce

  1 lb. spaghettini, cooked
1/2 lb. butter, at room temperature
  3 cloves garlic, finely minced
  1 tsp. salt

1/2 cup freshly grated
     parmesan cheese
     freshly ground black pepper

Cream together butter, garlic and salt until smooth. When pasta is al dente, drain well and turn into warm, buttered serving dish. Quickly mix in garlic butter and grated cheese. Serve in warm dishes and sprinkle pepper.

Note: 1/4 c. of chopped parsley, green onion or basil may be added to garlic butter.

Pickled Mushrooms and Onions

1/3 cup cider vinegar
1/3 cup salad oil
  1 small onion, sliced thin
  1 tsp. salt
  2 tsp. dried parsley flakes

1 tsp. prepared mustard
1 tsp. brown sugar
1 pt. mushrooms
  (approximately 2 cups or
  about 1/2 lb.)

In small saucepan, combine all ingredients except mushrooms. Bring to boil, add mushrooms, bring to second boil. Simmer 5-6 minutes. Chill several hours or overnight.

Lemon Green Beans

1	lb. fresh green beans, trimmed	finely slivered zest of 1 lemon
1/4	cup chicken or vegetable stock	pepper to taste
	juice of 1 lemon	fresh chopped parsley
4	Tbsp. (1/2 stick) unsalted butter	

Steam beans till crisp and tender. Rinse under cold water and drain. Combine stock and lemon juice in large skillet. Heat to boiling. Boil till reduced by half, about 4 minutes. Add butter, stir until smooth. Add beans and lemon zest. Toss till warmed through, about 2 minutes. Add pepper to taste. Sprinkle with parsley and serve.

Stuffed Zucchini

3	medium zucchini	1 cup (4 oz) shredded Monterey Jack cheese
2	Tbsp. butter	
1	cup chopped fresh mushrooms	2 Tbsp. chopped pimento (optional)
2	Tbsp. flour	
1/4	tsp. dried oregano, crushed	1/4 cup grated Parmesan cheese

Cook whole zucchini in boiling salted water about 10 minutes or until tender. Drain. Cut in half lengthwise. Scoop out centers (save), leaving a 1/4 inch shell. Chop center portion and set aside.

Melt butter in a large skillet; saute mushrooms until tender. Stir in flour and oregano; remove from heat. Stir in Monterey Jack cheese and pimento; stir in the reserved chopped zucchini. Heat mixture through.

Preheat broiler. Fill zucchini shells, using about 1/4 cup filling for each. Sprinkle with parmesan cheese. Broil several inches from source of heat until hot and bubbly.

Note: May be assembled in advance, covered and refrigerated up to 4 hours.

Creamy Broccoli Bake

2 pkg. frozen broccoli spears/chunks	1/2 cup shredded cheddar cheese
1 can cream of mushroom soup	1 cup Bisquick
1/4 cup milk	1/4 cup firm margarine

Cook frozen broccoli as desired. Drain well. Place broccoli in baking dish. Heat oven to 400 degrees.

Beat soup and milk until smooth. Pour over broccoli. Sprinkle with cheese. Mix Bisquick and margarine until crumbly. Spread over cheese. Bake until crumbs are light brown, about 20 minutes.

Saute Spinach

1 bunch fresh spinach	dash of salt
3 slices bacon	dash of black pepper
1 clove finely chopped garlic	dash of nutmeg
1/2 cup chopped onions	

Blanch cleaned spinach leaves in boiling water. Remove immediately to ice bath. Drain well. Saute bacon, add onions when bacon is half done, add garlic, salt, pepper and nutmeg. (Careful with the nutmeg - a little goes a long way). Add spinach and saute until hot. Serve immediately.

Basque Potatoes

3	lbs. small new white or red potatoes	1/2	tsp. dried thyme
6	Tbsp. unsalted butter	1/2	tsp. minced fresh or crushed dried rosemary
3	Tbsp. olive oil	1/2	tsp. paprika
3	large garlic cloves, crushed through a press		dash of cayenne pepper
1/2	cup chopped fresh parsley	1/2	tsp. salt
		1/4	tsp. freshly ground black pepper

Preheat oven to 375 degrees. Scrub the potatoes well, and pat dry. In a large roasting pan, melt the butter in the oil over moderate heat. Add the garlic, parsley, thyme, rosemary, paprika and cayenne. Add the potatoes and roll them in the seasoned butter to coat well. Bake, basting the potatoes occasionally with the butter, for about 40 minutes, or until the potatoes are tender. Season with the salt and black pepper.

Notes

Main Dishes

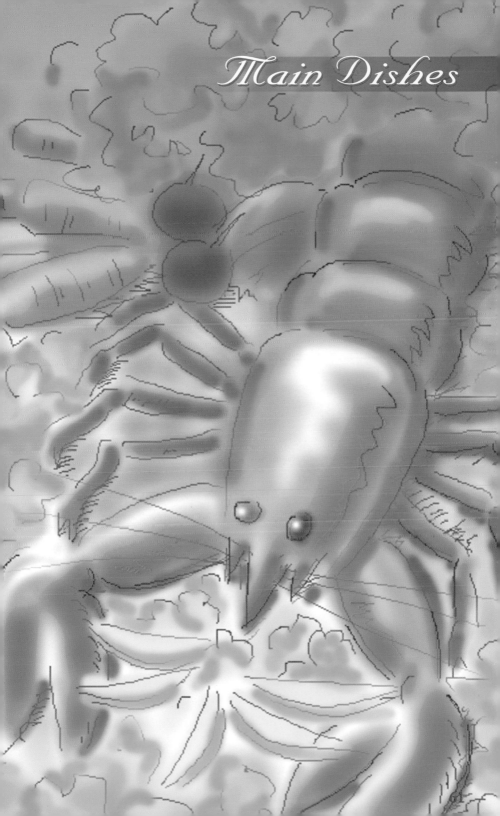

Main Dishes

Saffron Risotto with Shrimp and Scallop

by "3660 on the Rise"

1	tsp. shallots	3-4	cups clam or fish stock
1/2	medium onion		shrimps
1	Tbsp. olive oil		scallops
1/4	tsp. saffron	2	Tbsp. butter
1/2	cup white wine	1	Tbsp. parmesan cheese grated fine
1/2	cup arborio rice (Italian Rice)		salt and pepper

Saute shallots and onion with olive oil. Add saffron, white wine and reduce by half. Add rice and cook for about 2 minutes stirring constantly so rice will not burn.

Add stock and simmer for about 16 minutes, stirring once and a while. Rice should be al dente and not mushy. Add shrimp and scallop after 13 minutes of cooking the rice. Add butter, cheese and season with salt and pepper.

For a different flavor, you can sear seafood first before adding it to the risotto.

Shrimp with Black Bean Sauce

1	lb. medium shrimp	1	Tbsp. cornstarch
2	cloves garlic, minced	2	Tbsp. chicken broth
1	Tbsp. black beans, rinsed	2	tsp. sugar
3	Tbsp. peanut oil	1	tsp. oyster sauce
1/2	tsp. salt	2	tsp. shoyu
1	cup chicken broth		Chinese parsley

Peel and devein shrimp. Saute garlic and mashed black beans in oil for 1 minute. Add shrimp and salt. Saute until shrimp turns pink. Add chicken broth, cornstarch dissolved in chicken broth (2 Tbsp.), sugar, oyster sauce and shoyu. Stir and simmer sauce is translucent. Garnish with Chinese parsley.

Sake Glazed Shrimp with Hong Kong Noodles

by 3660 On the Rise

2	Tbsp. oil	1/2	cup red onion, chopped
28	pcs. shrimp, peeled and deveined	1/2	cup sake
	salt and pepper	1	cup teriyaki sauce, slightly
1	tsp. garlic, chopped		thickened with cornstarch
1/2	cup red bell pepper,		- see recipe
	cut into 1/2" squares		chow mein noodles
1/2	cup green bell pepper,	1	cup green onion, cut
	cut into 1/2" squares		diagonally to garnish
		1	tsp. toasted sesame seeds

In a large saute pan, heat 2 Tbsp. oil. Add shrimp and saute on one side. Season with salt and pepper. Turn over shrimp and season. Add garlic and toss. Add bell peppers and red onions and stir. Fry until shrimp is done. Deglaze with sake and add teriyaki sauce. Cook slightly. Place shrimp on crisp noodles and pour sauce over. Garnish with green onion and toasted sesame seeds.

Teriyaki Sauce:

1/4	cup sugar	1	cup mirin
1/4	cup sake		cornstarch mixed with
1/2	cup shoyu		water to make paste

Heat sugar, sake, shoyu, & mirin until dissolved. Thicken with cornstarch.

To prepare noodles:

In large sauce pan, heat 2 inches of oil. Loosen the noodle bundles (chow mein) and frying in oil until crips. Turn over and fry again until crisp. Drain on paper towel.

Fried Shrimp

1   lb. shrimp
2   Tbsp. oil
2   stalks green onion

Sauce:

2   Tbsp. shoyu
1   Tbsp. wine

1   Tbsp. sugar
1   tsp. sesame oil
1/8   tsp. salt

Wash and clean shrimp without removing shells. Soak shrimps in sauce for 30 minutes. To heated pan, add the oil, green onions and drained shrimp. As shrimp turn red, pour sauce into pan to thicken. Serve immediately.

Teriyaki Shrimp

2   lbs. shrimp
1/3   cup shoyu
1/4   cup sugar

1   clove garlic, crushed
1   small piece ginger root, crushed
1/4   tsp. ajinomoto

Wash shrimp, remove legs but not shell. To butterfly shrimp, cut back of each shrimp length wise through the shell to flatten; remove vein. In a flat dish, combine remaining ingredients. Place shrimp with shell side up in shoyu mixture; marinate 45 minutes or longer. Place shrimp on rack of broiler pan with shell side down; broil 3 inches from unit in electric oven for 3-4 minutes. Turn and broil 2 more minutes. Makes 6 servings.

Grilled Shrimp

with a Tofu & Vegetable Cake, and
Tomato Shrimp Avocado Salsa
by 3660 On the Rise

Tofu Cake:

    1   pkg. firm tofu - drained and mashed
    2   eggs
  1/4   cup bell pepper - diced
  1/4   cup celery
  1/4   cup onion
    1   tsp. ginger - grated
    1   tsp. garlic - chopped

Place all ingredients in a large bowl and mix thoroughly. Form into patties. Pan fry on medium high heat for approximately 3 minutes on each side.

Tomato Shrimp Avocado Salsa

    1   avocado - diced
    1   tomato - diced
  1/4   red onion - diced
  1/4   cup chopped cilantro
  1/2   cup bay shrimp meat
    2   Tbsp. rice wine vinegar
        salt and pepper to taste

Mix all ingredients. Set aside.

12 Large Shrimps

On each skewer place 3 shrimps and grill. Place tofu cake on platter, then place grilled shrimp on top. Spoon salsa over shrimp.

Shrimp Creole

1 lb. medium size shrimp, shelled and deveined
2 Tbsp. butter
1/2 tsp. paprika
1 cup chopped round onion
1 clove garlic, chopped

1 cup chopped green pepper (2 cup fresh asparagus may be used as substitute)
1 can stewed tomatoes (16 oz.)
salt and fresh ground pepper to taste

In a saucepan large enough to hold all the ingredients, melt butter and add paprika and stir until well blended. Add onion, garlic and green pepper; simmer until tender. Add tomatoes, salt and fresh ground pepper. Bring to boil for 5 minutes. Lower heat and add shrimp, simmer for 3 more minutes or until shrimp are firm and pink.

Great served over freshly cooked white rice or spaghetti. Makes 4 servings.

Open-faced Crab Sandwich

1 can Geisha crab
3 Tbsp. mayonnaise
4 Tbsp. green onions
handful sliced olives

handful mozzarella cheese, grated
salt and pepper, to taste
paprika
English muffin

Mix all ingredients except paprika and spread on English muffin. Sprinkle with paprika. Broil until cheese melts or browned.

Curried Crab

2	whole dungeness crabs	1	onion, chopped
3	Tbsp. salad oil	1/2	cup sliced celery
1/4	lb. ground pork	1	can chicken broth (13 3/4 oz)
2	cloves garlic, crushed	2	Tbsp. cornstarch
1	tsp. salt	3	Tbsp. water
1	tsp. sugar	1	egg, slightly beaten
3	Tbsp. curry powder	3	green onion stalks, chopped

Thaw crabs, rinse, disjoint. Using the flat side of a wide knife or kitchen scissors, crack/cut shells, but do not remove meat.

Heat oil in wok. Add pork and cook on high heat stirring constantly until browned. Add garlic, salt, sugar, curry powder, onion and celery. Stir fry 2 to 3 minutes. Add crab and broth. Cook 3 minutes, stirring. Combine cornstarch with water, stir into crab mixture and cook 1 minute. Add beaten egg and cook 2 minutes. Sprinkle with green onions before serving.

Dungeness Crab

in Garlic, Butter & Vermouth Sauce

1/2	cup butter (melted)	1	tsp. shoyu
1	cup vermouth	1	tsp. sugar
1	14 oz. can of chicken broth	1	Tbsp. lemon juice
2	Tbsp. minced garlic	2-3	fresh Dungeness crab
2	Tbsp. minced parsley		(cooked and cracked)

Combine all ingredients except crab and bring to a boil. Add cracked crab. Heat thoroughly. Serve immediately.

Sesame Grilled Kona Crab Hash

with Black Bean, Tomato & Fennel Cream
by Gary Strehl, Executive Chef Hawaii Prince Hotel

2	tsp. garlic (minced)	1	whole egg
1/2	lb. wild mushrooms (diced 1/2")	2	Tbsp. chili pepper (fresh ground)
1	red roasted bell pepper (diced)	1	tsp. sesame oil
3	Tbsp. olive oil	1/2	tsp. worcestershire sauce
1	Tbsp. whole butter	1/2	tsp. fresh ground pepper
1-1/2	cups Kona crab meat (may be substituted with snow crab or Dungeness)	1/2	cup heavy cream juice of 1 lime
4	medium red potatoes (steamed and diced)	1/2	cup bread crumbs (ground)
2	Tbsp. Dijon mustard	2	Tbsp. roasted sesame seed
3	tsp. cilantro (chopped)	1/2	cup wild rice
		1/4	cup cornbread crumbs

Saute garlic, mushrooms and bell peppers in olive oil and place into a stainless steel bowl. Add remaining ingredients, mix well and chill. Form into desired shape and using a hot saute pan, brown the crab well, outside should be crispy. Set hash onto plate and spoon black bean sauce and tomato sauce on either side. Spoon fennel cream over the center and garnish with cilantro.

Tomato Concasse

4	med. tomatoes (peeled, seeded and diced)	2	Tbsp. olive oil
1	tsp. shallots	1/2	tsp. garlic (minced)

Saute garlic, shallots and tomatoes in olive oil quickly and hold.

Continued on next page

Sesame Grilled Kona Crab Hash (continued from previous page)

Black Bean Sauce

1/2	tsp. ginger (minced)		juice of 1/2 lime
1	tsp. garlic (minced)	1	cup water
1/2	cup black beans	1	tsp. sugar
	(salted, rinsed)	1/2	tsp. sesame oil
2	Tbsp. peanut oil	1	Tbsp. tomato puree
2	cubes fish bouillon	1	Tbsp. cornstarch
1	tsp. oyster sauce		(mixed with water)
1	tsp. soy sauce		
	chili pepper to taste		

Saute ginger, garlic and black beans in peanut oil. Add fish bouillon, oyster sauce, soy sauce and chili pepper and simmer. Add lime, water, sugar, sesame oil and tomato puree. Thicken lightly with cornstarch and hold.

Fennel Cream

1	med. onion (sliced julienne)	1	Tbsp. pernod
1	tsp. garlic (minced)	1	cup fish stock
1	cup fresh fennel	1	bay leaf
	(steamed and cut julienne)	1/4	tsp. white pepper
2	Tbsp. olive oil	1	cup heavy cream

Saute onions, garlic and fennel until translucent in olive oil. Add pernod, fish stock, bay leaf and white pepper. Add heavy cream and reduce by 1/2.

Luxurious Crab and Artichoke Casserole

3 Tbsp. butter	1/3 cup fresh crab meat
1 Tbsp. minced onion	1 9 oz. package frozen
3 Tbsp. flour	artichoke hearts, cooked
1/3 cup cream, heated to	7/8 cup shell macaroni, cooked
boiling point	and drained
3 Tbsp. madeira	2/3 cup grated Gruyere or
salt and pepper	Swiss cheese
2 tsp. lemon juice	paprika (optional)

Preheat oven to 350 degrees. Melt butter in a large, heavy pan. When butter sizzles, add onion and saute until golden. Stir in flour, cook over low heat until flour is pale yellow. Remove from heat. Add cream, stirring vigorously. Return to moderate heat and stir until sauce comes to a boil. Reduce heat and add madeira. Season with salt and pepper.

Pour lemon juice over crab meat and toss lightly. Combine crab, artichoke hearts, macaroni and sauce together in a buttered 2 qt. casserole dish. Sprinkle with cheese and dust with paprika, if desired. Bake 15-20 minutes or until heated through.

Serves 4 to 6 people.

Katsuo Miso Yaki (Aku)

3/4 cup miso	1/4 cup sugar
1 tsp. grated ginger	1-2 lbs. aku, sliced 1/2" thick
1/4 cup sake	

Mix ingredients and soak overnight or longer. (Fish soaked in sauce will keep 3 to 4 days if kept in covered dish and refrigerated).

Broil and serve.

Slipper Lobster Brochette

with Fresh Lychee, Roasted Red Pepper & Mango - Basil Coulis
by Roger Dikon - Maui Prince Hotel

1	spaghetti squash	4	bamboo skewers
1	roasted red bell pepper	1/2	oz. Limu Wa'wae Iole
12	fresh lychee fruits		(optional, for garnish
12	oz. Hawaiian slipper lobster		only)
	tail meat, cut into 1"chunks		

Cut the spaghetti squash in half and remove the seeds. Bake 350 degrees or steam until cooked and sliced with a fork. Set aside. Roast one red bell pepper over an open flame until charred and put into a paper bag until the skin wilts (about 5 minutes), then run under cold water to wash away the skin. Cut into 1" squares. Peel and seed the fresh lychee fruit, keeping it as intact as possible. Prepare the mango coulis and basil vinaigrette sauces.

Skewer the lobster meat alternately with the lychee and roasted pepper equally. When ready to serve, steam or grill the lobster-lychee brochette until just cooked, leaving the lobster slightly opaque in the center. Set the brochette on the squash and garnish with the mango coulis, basil vinaigrette and the limu Wa'wae Iole on the side for color.

Mango Coulis

1	cup mango pulp	1	Tbsp. lemon juice
1/3	cup Hawaiian raw sugar syrup		

Blend all ingredients. Strain to remove any lumps.

Basil Vinaigrette

50	fresh basil leaves	3	Tbsp. white wine vinegar
2	cloves garlic		fresh ground pepper
9	Tbsp. macadamia nut oil		and salt to taste

Blend all ingredients in blender or food processor.

Fresh Island Fish Steam-Baked in Paper

with Manila Butter Clams, Shiitake Mushrooms, Mango, Mint & Lime

by Roger Dikon - Maui Prince Hotel

4	15" x 15" sheets paper or foil	1	Tbsp. butter
8	Shiitake mushrooms, thinly sliced	1	mango, sliced
		1/2	cup chopped fresh mint
1	onion, sliced	1	lime, sliced into 8 slices
1	carrot, julienne	2	Tbsp. dry vermouth
4	6 oz. fish filets		
12	Manila clams		

Fold the 4 pieces of paper in half and cut out a large half-heart shape, keeping the fold in middle. Lightly butter one side of the paper and divide the mushrooms, onions and carrots evenly between them on the buttered side. Place a piece of fish and 3 clams on top of the vegetables with 1 Tbsp. butter and lay 1/4 of the sliced mango on top. Sprinkle freshly chopped mint and place two thin slices of lime over it, then drizzle 1/2 tsp. of dry vermouth.

Fold the paper over the fish, leaving a 1-2 inch space between the edge of the paper and the fish. Starting at the top of the heart, crimp and firmly fold the cut edges to the inside so no steam can escape.

Bake on a pan in a pre-heated 450-degree oven for 10 to 12 minutes. When done, the paper will be puffed and lightly browned.

To serve, cut a slice in the top and fold back or cut the side and slide the fish and vegetables on to the plate.

Makes 4 servings.

Pan Fried Ulua

Green Papaya and Shrimp Relish, Lime Butter Sauce
by 3660 on the Rise

1/2	cup green papaya grated into match sticks			patis to taste
				salt and pepper to taste
1/8	cup bell pepper, julienne	1/4	cup bay shrimp
1/8	cup red onion, julienne	4	6 oz. ulua fillets
1/8	cup tsp. grated ginger	4	Tbsp. peanut oil
1/4	cup sugar		flour (to coat fillets)
1/4	cup rice wine vinegar		

Combine papaya, bell pepper, onion and ginger in a large bowl and reserve on the side. In another bowl add sugar, vinegar and patis and stir till sugar dissolves. Toss vinegar mixture with the green papaya. Season with salt and pepper. Add shrimp and mix.

Lime Butter Sauce

3	lime (juice and zest)	1	tsp. chopped shallots
1/4	cup rice wine vinegar	1/4	cup heavy cream
1/4	cup white wine	1/2	cup butter cut into pieces
1/8	cup shoyu		

In a sauce pot simmer lime juice, vinegar, white wine, shoyu and shallots. Reduce by 1/2 and add cream. Reduce by half till cream thickens. Remove from heat and slowly add butter whisking constantly till smooth. Strain through a fine sieve and add lime zest. Season with salt and pepper to taste.

Season the fish with salt and pepper. Dredge in flour and saute with in a hot pan with peanut oil. Sear one side till brown and turn to brown other side till fish is done.

Place fish on plate, sauce with lime butter sauce and top with green papaya salad.

Fish and Spinach Bake

Fish fillets
1 pkg. frozen chopped spinach

chopped onions
mayonnaise

Season fish fillets and place in a baking dish.

Defrost spinach and mix with onions and mayonnaise. Spread over fish and bake 350 degrees until cooked through.

Baked Curry Mahi

1-4 lbs. mahimahi (sliced)
1 tsp. salt
1 tsp. pepper
1/2 lb. shredded mozzarella cheese

1/2 lb. shredded cheddar cheese
(or any cheese of your choice)
2 Tbsp. curry powder
1 can cream of mushroom soup
1 tsp. paprika

Lightly grease 9" x 13" baking pan. Salt and pepper mahi to taste. Lay in baking pan. Spread mozzarella and cheddar cheeses over fish. Sprinkle curry powder over cheese. Spread cream of mushroom soup over top. Sprinkle paprika for color. Bake at 350 degrees for 30 minutes. (May use same recipes substituting chicken.)

Miso Salmon

8 slices salmon
1/2 cup miso
1/2 cup sugar

2 tsp. salt
5 Tbsp. honey
2 Tbsp. mirin

Combine all ingredients except fish; mix well. Spread a layer of miso mixture in covered dish and lay the pieces of fish on it. Spread remaining miso mixture over fish. Marinate at least 24 hours. Broil 3 to 5 minutes on each side.

Indigo Salmon Cakes

by Glenn Chu - Indigo Restaurant

Salmon Patties:

1/2 lb. fresh salmon, skinned and boned	1 Tbsp. kaffir lime leaf, finely minced
1/4 cup green bell peppers, finely diced	1/4 fresh lime juice
1/4 cup red bell peppers, finely diced	1 cup mayonnaise
	6 Tbsp. chives, chopped
1/4 cup Maui onion, finely diced	2 Tbsp. salt and pepper to taste

Breading:

1 egg, beaten	2 Tbsp. vegetable oil
2 cups panko (or bread crumbs)	

Sauce:

1/2 cup mayonnaise	2 Tbsp. chives, chopped
1/2 cup sour cream	salt and pepper to taste
2 Tbsp. Chipolte chile sauce	

Chop salmon until smooth or place in a food processor. In a bowl, mix the salmon, peppers, onions, lime leaves and juice, mayonnaise, chives, salt and pepper. Form 3 oz. patties about 4" round. Dip patties into the egg wash, then dredge and cover with panko. Heat skillet to medium-high with vegetable oil and brown patties on each side, for about 5 minutes. Blend the mayonnaise, sour cream, chile sauce, chives, salt and pepper until smooth. Assemble cakes on a bed of lettuce with plenty of Chipolte sauce on the side and garnish with Chinese parsley (optional).

Makes 8 cakes.

Poached Salmon Fillets

with Dill Sauce
Sauce:

6 Tbsp. finely chopped dill pickles	1 Tbsp. fresh lemon juice
3 Tbsp. chopped fresh dill	1 cup sour cream
	salt and pepper

Place pickles, dill and juice in small bowl and stir sour cream in gently just until combined; do not overmix or sauce will thin out. Season to taste with salt and pepper. (Can be made 2 days ahead. Cover and chill).

Salmon:

3 8 oz. bottles clam juice or vegetable broth	10 whole peppercorns
3 cup dry white wine or cooking wine	8 (6 to 8 oz.) salmon fillets
	8 fresh dill sprigs
	6 lemon slices

Combine first 3 ingredients in large, deep skillet; bring to simmer over medium heat. Simmer 5 minutes. Reduce heat to medium-low. Add half of salmon, cover and simmer until just cooked through...(the key to salmon is to remove it from the heat when it is 75% done). Transfer to platter. Repeat with remaining salmon. Cover salmon; chill until cold. (Can be made 1 day ahead).

Line platter with lettuce. Top with salmon. Garnish with lemon slices and dill sprigs. Serve with sauce.

Barbecued Salmon

3/4 cup apple cider	1 large garlic clove, crushed through a press
6 Tbsp. shoyu	2 salmon fillets, 2 1/2 to 3 pounds each
2 Tbsp. unsalted butter	

In a small saucepan, combine the cider and shoyu. Bring to a boil over high heat, then reduce the heat to moderate and simmer for three minutes. Add the butter and garlic and continue cooking, stirring occasionally, until the liquid thickens enough to coat the back of a spoon, about twenty minutes. Remove the marinade from the heat. Let cool to room temperature.

Continued on next page

Barbecued Salmon (continued from previous page)

Pat the salmon fillets dry and place them skin-side down on a rack. Brush the marinade evenly over the salmon. Let stand at room temperature for thirty minutes.

Preheat the broiler. Place the salmon, skin-side down, on a well-oiled broiler rack and broil about 6 inches from the heat until the top is glazed and the fish is still slightly translucent in the center, 12 to 15 minutes. Serve garnished with parsley and lemon slices if desired.

Serves 8 people.

Pan Fried Potato Crusted Salmon

Wild Mushroom and Spinach Broth
by "3660 On the Rise"

4	salmon fillets 6 oz. each	1/2	cup button mushrooms
	salt and pepper to taste	3	cups veal stock
2	baker potatoes	14	leaves cleaned and
1/4	cup bacon finely diced		stemmed spinach
1	Tbsp. shallot chopped	1	tomato, seeded and diced
1	garlic clove coarsely chopped	2	Tbsp. butter
1/4	cup white wine	3	Tbsp. salad oil
1	cup wild mushrooms		salt and pepper
	(porcini, chanterelles,		
	shiitakes, morels, etc)		

Season salmon with salt and pepper.. Peel potato and put through a vegetable noodle machine. Blanch potato noodles in hot water for about 4 minutes. Cool immediately with ice water. Drain potato noodle and wrap around salmon and reserve on the side.

Saute bacon in sauce pan over medium heat till medium cooked. Add shallots and garlic and saute for a minute. Add wine and mushrooms and cook for about 5 minutes. Add stock and simmer till stock reduces down by half. Add spinach and tomato. Simmer for another 2 minutes and finish with butter. Season with salt and pepper.

Heat frying pan with a little oil. Add potato crushed salmon and saute till golden brown on one side and turn cook till a golden brown. Ladle sauce on the bottom of the plate, place cooked salmon on sauce.

Roy's Green Tea Risotto with Spicy Salmon

by Roy Yamaguchi

Risotto:

1	Tbsp. olive oil	2	cups medium grain rice
1/8	cup bacon		(half cooked)
1	tsp. minced shallots	2 1/2	cups chicken stock
1/4	tsp. minced ginger	1	Tbsp. green tea powder
1/4	tsp. minced garlic	1/3	cup shredded parmesan
3/4	cup shiitake mushrooms,		cheese
	sliced	1	Tbsp. butter

In a wok or skillet, heat olive oil and saute bacon, shallots, ginger and garlic till golden brown then add shiitake mushrooms. Add rice, chicken stock and green tea powder and cook for about 3 to 5 minutes over medium heat. Add shredded parmesan cheese and cook until cheese is melted. Lastly, add butter and stir.

Salmon:

4	3 oz. salmon fillet		hichimi pepper
	salt	1	tsp. olive oil

Season salmon with salt, pepper and olive oil and saute in a heated saute pan for 45 seconds to 1 minute on each side.

Plate:

Place risotto on the bottom of a plate. Place salmon fillet on top of the risotto. Sprinkle hichimi pepper on risotto. Garnish with the following.

1/3   cup pickled ginger
1/2   cup julienne dried nori

Makes 4 servings.

Oyster with Spinach in Cream

12 oysters in shell
 3 Tbsp. margarine
 1 celery stalk, minced
 2 garlic cloves, chopped
 2 Tbsp. parsley,
      finely chopped

3-4 cups fresh spinach, chopped
     salt and pepper to taste
 1   slice bread, torn into
      small pieces
4-5 Tbsp. heavy cream
 1   tsp. lemon juice

Grill or broil oysters until shell pops open (about 5-10 minutes). Remove meat from shell and set aside along with liquid. Wash 12 half shells and set aside.

Heat margarine in medium sized pan or pot. When hot, add celery, garlic and parsley, and stir fry 1 minute. Add spinach and season with salt and pepper. Stir together, cover, and continue cooking until spinach wilts. Mix in bread and cream; cook until cream just bubbles. Turn off heat and cover.

In small sauce pan, heat remaining margarine and add oyster meat with 1 Tbsp. liquid and the lemon juice. Cook 2 minutes.

Place oyster meat in shells and top with spinach mixture. Serve warm with lemon wedges.

Serves 2 people.

Tofu with Lomi Salmon

1/2 lb. salted salmon
 3   tomatoes, diced
 1   Japanese cucumber, cubed

 1   medium onion, chopped
 5   stalks green onion, chopped
 1   tofu, drained and diced

Soak salmon in water for 3 hours. Remove skin and bones and shred. Combine salmon, tomatoes, cucumber and onions, mix well. Finally, add tofu; mix carefully. Chill thoroughly before serving.

Cornmeal Crusted Calamari

with Creole Mustard Sauce
By 3660 On the Rise

4   5-6 oz. calamari steak, pounded
    out with meat tenderizer
1   cup milk   salt and pepper to taste
1   cup cornmeal   1/4   cup clarified butter

Place calamari steak on a cutting board and pound with a meat tenderizer. Place in a bowl with milk. Mix salt, pepper and cornmeal in a flat pan. Coat both sides of the calamari with cornmeal. Saute in clarified butter over medium high heat. Place on plate and pour sauce on each.

Creole Mustard Sauce:

1   Tbsp. shallot, minced   2   Tbsp. creole mustard
1/2   cup white wine   1   Tbsp. capers
1   Tbsp. L & P sauce   4   oz. unsalted butter, cubed
1/4   cup heavy cream

Put shallots, white wine and L & P sauce in a sauce pan, reduce by one half. Add heavy cream, mustard and capers. Reduce heat to low. Whisk in butter, one cube at a time. Keep warm in a double boiler.

Lau Lau, Lazy Style

8   Ti leaves
4   lbs. taro leaves
3   lbs. pork butt, cut into 1" x 1" chunks
1   lb. salted butterfish, cut into small pieces

Line a large baking pan with foil. Lay 4 ti leaves in pan. Wash and discard stems from taro leaves. Use half of taro leaves over the ti leaves. Arrange pork and fish evenly. Place remaining taro leaves and ti leaves on top. Cover pan with foil. Bake at 350 degrees for 3 hours.
Optional: Sweet potatoes may be added before covering with ti leaves.

Roy's Hot Citrus Sauce Mahimahi

topped with Kea'au Bananas and Macadamia Nuts
by Roy Yamaguchi

Bananas:

1	banana	1/8	tsp. hichimi pepper
1/8	tsp. sugar	2	tsp. coconut flakes

Slice banana in half lengthwise and into thirds crosswise, sprinkle with sugar, hichimi pepper and coconut flakes. Saute bananas, coconut side down first, for 1 minute on each side.

Sauce:

2	cups water	1/3	cup sugar
1 1/2	Tbsp. crushed peppercorns		

In a sauce pan put water, crushed peppercorns and sugar and reduce for 5 minutes or until a syrup consistency.

Add the following to the reduction and reserve.

2	Tbsp. honey	1/2	Tbsp. orange zest
1/2	Tbsp. lemon zest	2	Tbsp. orange juice
3	Tbsp. lilikoi		concentrate
	(passion fruit) syrup	1	Tbsp. canola oil
1-1/2	Tbsp. lemon juice		
1/4	cup orange juice		

Mahimahi:

4	8 oz. mahimahi fillets	1	tsp. canola oil
	salt		

Season mahimahi fillets with salt and saute for about 2 minutes on each side with 1 teaspoon of canola oil.

Plate:

1/2	cup baby greens	1/4	cup julienne cucumbers
1 1/2	Tbsp. chopped roasted macadamia nuts		

Place 1/2 cup baby greens on plate. Place mahimahi on top of greens. Place a banana on top of each piece of mahimahi then drizzle 2 oz. sauce around mahimahi. Garnish with julienne cucumbers and chopped roasted macadamia nuts.

Makes 4 servings.

Chicken on a Sunday

5 lbs. chicken	1 1/2 cups wild rice
1 can cream of mushroom soup	1 cup milk
1 can cream of celery soup	1 pkg. onion soup mix

Place chicken in a large pan. Mix together soups, rice, milk and onion soup mix. Pour over chicken and cover with tin foil, bake 325 degrees for 2 1/4 hours.

General Snyder's Chicken Casserole

1 large broccoli (chopped)	2/3 cup mayonnaise
3 cups diced chicken	1 block of butter
1 egg (beaten)	1/2 pkg. shredded
1 can cream of celery soup	cheddar cheese
2 cans cream of chicken soup	1 pkg. stuffing
1 tsp. lemon juice	

Spread broccoli over bottom of greased casserole dish. Spread chicken over broccoli. Combine egg, soups, mayonnaise and lemon juice in bowl. Mix and pour over chicken. Sprinkle cheese. Melt butter and toss over stuffing. Spread stuffing over top and bake at 350 degrees for one hour.

Optional: Use leftover turkey instead of chicken.

Chicken Parmesan

5   lbs. chicken (thighs, breasts, drumsticks or split broilers)
       washed and drained well, sprinkle lightly with salt
2   cups mayonnaise
1   cup grated Parmesan cheese
1   Tbsp. garlic powder
4   tsp. oregano flakes
2   tsp. poultry seasoning
1   Tbsp. fresh parsley - chopped

Mix above ingredients together well except chicken. Dredge chicken pieces in mayonnaise mixture making sure chicken pieces are well coated. Lay chicken on a wire rack lined baking pan. Bake at 300 degrees for 1 hours or until chicken is well done.

Roast Chicken Jardiniere

1   roasting chicken   onions, chopped
    carrots, chopped   4   cups chicken stock
    celery, chopped   2   tbsp. butter
    leeks, chopped   1   clove garlic finely chopped

Dry chicken, season with salt and pepper. Roast on rack in oven preheated to 325 degrees for 1 hour. Let stand for 1 hour to cool before deboning.

Cut carrots, celery, leeks and onions in equal amounts and blanche in 4 cups chicken stock for 3 to 5 minutes. Drain. Saute vegetables in hot butter for 3 to 4 minutes, add garlic and continue cooking for a few more minutes. Pour over deboned chicken and finish in a 300 degrees oven for 15 minutes.

Cornish Hen
with Garlic & Mustard

1   cornish hen split in half
1/2   cup marmalade or apricot jam
2   cloves garlic, minced
2   Tbsp. Dijon mustard

In a small bowl combine jam, minced garlic and mustard. Place cornish hen in a ziplock plastic bag and add the jam mixture. Refrigerate hen for 4 hours, turning occasionally.

Place 2 cornish hen halves, cut side down in baking pan lined with foil. Bake uncovered for 45 minutes at 350 degrees on middle rack. If the top of the hen begins to darken excessively, drape with foil until baking is completed.

Delicious Chicken Adobo

3   lb. chicken, cut up into pieces

Marinade Sauce:

2   cloves garlic, minced   2   Tbsp. brown sugar
1   bay leaf   1/2   cup cider vinegar
1   tsp. cracked black peppercorn   1/2   cup shoyu

Mix marinade sauce ingredients together. Add chicken and soak for 2 hours. Simmer chicken in sauce for 30 to 45 minutes. Serve with hot rice.

Miso Chicken

by Hari Kojima - Hari's Kitchen

1 carton white miso, 27 oz.	1/2 tsp. sesame oil
1/4 cup chives	water to taste
1/3 cup white vinegar	5 lbs. chicken thighs
3 Tbsp. sugar	or IQF wings
1/4 cup shoyu	

Combine all ingredients except water and chicken. Mix well. Add a little water at a time to secure proper texture and thickness of mixture (you may not desire to change it, however). If using frozen chicken thighs, thaw, debone and butterfly (so it can lay flat). If using frozen chicken wings, just thaw and use. Put chicken pieces in large bowl along with marinade and mix well. Leave in refrigerator for 2 hours. Using a covered type charcoal grill, cover (leaving all vents open) and cook on one side. Turn over, cook more covering again. Start eating! An excellent dish for tailgating, pot luck or just family get togethers.

Oyster Sauce Chicken on Noodles

2 lbs. chicken breast	2 cups broccoli
1 Tbsp. soy sauce	1/2 cup oyster sauce
1/4 cup flour	1 Tbsp. sugar
2 pkgs. chow mein noodles	1 can chicken broth
1 Tbsp. salad oil	1 Tbsp. cornstarch
2 cloves garlic, minced	1 tsp. water

Cut chicken into pieces and mix with soy sauce. Coat chicken with flour. Heat noodles in 250 degree oven for 10 minutes. Brown garlic in oil and discard garlic. Fry chicken in wok and remove. Stir fry broccoli, then add chicken oyster sauce, sugar and broth. Mix cornstarch with water and add to mixture. Serve over noodles.

Chicken with Wine Sauce

1 1/2 Tbsp. flour	1/2 lb. fresh mushrooms, sliced
1/2 tsp. salt	1/4 cup onion, chopped
1/8 tsp. pepper	1/4 cup parsley, chopped
2 large chicken breasts, boned and sliced	1 cup white wine
4 Tbsp. margarine	

Combine flour, salt and pepper. Coat chicken slices with flour mixture. Shake off and reserve excess flour.

Melt 2 Tbsp. margarine in skillet over medium heat. Brown chicken and remove from skillet. Add remaining margarine, mushrooms, onions and 2 Tbsp. parsley. Saute until onion is transparent. Remove from heat. Stir in reserved flour and blend in wine. Bring to boil. Add chicken. Cover, reduce heat and simmer 25 minutes or until tender.

Garnish with parsley.

Chiang Mai Chicken

3 lbs. chicken breasts, deboned	1/4 tsp. ground coriander
2 large cloves of garlic, chopped	14 tsp. coarsely ground pepper
1/4 cup thinly sliced green onions	2 Tbsp. fish sauce
1 Tbsp. chopped ginger	(nampla or nuoc nam)

Grind garlic, onion, ginger, coriander, pepper and fish sauce into a coarse paste. Rub paste over chicken, marinate 1/2 day or overnight. Broil chicken until meat is no longer pink (15-20 minutes). Turn as needed.

Indian Style BBQ Chicken

8 chicken breasts, deboned
1 cup non-fat yogurt
2 cloves garlic, minced or
     pressed
2 Tbsp. minced fresh ginger
1 fresh jalapeno chili,
     seeded & minced

2   tsp. ground coriander
1   Tbsp. sugar
1   tsp. ground cumin
1/2 tsp. ground cinnamon
2   whole cloves
1/2 - 1 tsp. cayenne to taste
     salt to taste

Mix all above ingredients except chicken in large bowl. Marinate chicken in this mixture. Cover and chill for 6 hours or until the next day. Cook chicken on a BBQ grill and baste with marinade. Grill chicken until meat is no longer pink (12-15 minutes).

Sweet Sour Chicken

4 lbs. chicken wings
2 eggs well-beaten
1 cup flour
   oil

Sauce:

3/4 cup sugar
1/2 cup vinegar
1/4 cup pineapple juice
1   tsp. ajinomoto

2   Tbsp. soy sauce
3   Tbsp. ketchup
1/2 tsp. salt

Cut wings in half and discard tips. Dip in beaten eggs and coat with flour. Deep fry until light brown. Put in shallow pan lined with foil. Mix sauce ingredients together. Pour sauce over wings and bake at 350 degrees for 30 minutes.

Sesame BBQ Chicken

4	lbs. chicken pieces	2	tsp. grated ginger
1	cup sugar	2	tsp. crushed garlic
1 1/2	cups shoyu	4	Tbsp. sesame oil
6	Tbsp. sake or wine	4	Tbsp. toasted sesame seeds
1	tsp. salt	2	stalks green onions, chopped

To make marinade, mix all ingredients except chicken. Marinate chicken pieces for several hours or overnight. Bake at 350 degrees in oven or grill over hibachi until fully cooked.

BBQ Chicken

5	lbs. chicken thighs	2	oz. mirin
1	clove garlic, grated	3/4	cup sugar
1	inch ginger, grated	1	tsp. salt
1/2	cup shoyu	1/2	cup ketchup

Blend all ingredients, except chicken, in a pan large enough to hold the chicken. Marinate chicken in sauce overnight. Bake in same pan at 350 degrees for one hour.

Huli-Huli Style Chicken

4 split broiler chicken

Marinade:

1/2	tsp. garlic salt	1	Tbsp. sugar
1/2	tsp. Hawaiian salt	6	cloves garlic, minced
4	Tbsp. shoyu	1	tsp. paprika
2	Tbsp. sesame oil		

Combine marinade ingredients. Soak chicken in marinade for 1 hour. Grill or smoke chicken until done.

Teriyaki Chicken

1	cup flour	1/2	cup shoyu
2	Tbsp. cornstarch	4	cloves garlic
	Boneless chicken	1	Tbsp. sesame seeds
	oil	1	Tbsp. sesame seed oil
1/2	cup sugar		chili powder (optional)

Mix flour and cornstarch. Roll chicken in cornstarch/flour mixture. Fry in oil. Combine sugar, shoyu, garlic, sesame seeds and sesame seed oil to make dipping sauce. Add chili powder if desired.

Pineapple Chicken

3	lb. chicken thighs	2	Tbsp. Katakuriko (potato
2	Tbsp. sesame oil		starch)
1	can #1 crushed pineapple	1	tsp. salt
1/3	cup shoyu	3	Tbsp. sugar
1	cup water	2	Tbsp. mirin
1	tsp. grated ginger	1/2	cup green onion, chopped

Brown chicken in sesame oil. Add remaining ingredients except green onions. Simmer until tender. Sprinkle green onions over hot chicken before serving.

Oven Broiled Chicken

24 pcs. chicken (5-6 lbs of split broiler, thigh, etc)
  wash and drain well. Sprinkle lightly with salt
3/4 cup margarine - melted
1 tsp. white pepper
1 tsp. paprika
1 tsp. poultry seasoning

Combine margarine, pepper, paprika and poultry seasonings. Brush or dribble over chicken. Bake at 400 degrees for 40 to 50 minutes until brown and tender.

Oh So Easy Oven Fried Chicken

5 lbs. chicken (breasts, thighs, drumsticks or whole legs)

Wash chicken and drain well. Sprinkle chicken with salt - to your taste. Refrigerate chicken for 1 hour.

Mix together

1 cup flour
3/4 tsp. black pepper

1/2 tsp. poultry seasoning
1 Tbsp. garlic powder

Mix together

1/2 cup shoyu
1 medium size onion (slice
  into 1/2 inch wedges)

1/4 cup water

Dredge chicken pieces into flour mixture, shake off excess. Lay chicken pieces on rack lined pan. Bake 350 degrees for 45 minutes or until "golden" in color. Remove chicken and lay in a baking pan. Sprinkle shoyu water mixture over chicken. Spread onion slices on top of chicken. Cover pan tightly with foil. Bake 325 degrees for 25 to 30 minutes.

One inch thick pork chops or pork loin can be substituted for the chicken but should be lightly fried first and then baked.

Sabra's Chili

1 lb. lean ground meat	2 cans tomato sauce
1 round onion, chopped	2 tsp. salt
1 bell pepper, chopped	2 tsp. pepper
1 7 oz. Portuguese sausage, cut lengthwise and sliced	2-3 Tbsp. chili powder
	2-10 shakes chili pepper flakes
1 can kidney beans	2 bay leaves
2 cans whole tomatoes	

Brown ground meat, add onions and pepper. Add sausage, stir. Add beans, tomatoes, and tomato sauce. Adjust seasonings to your taste. Simmer 2 to 2 1/2 hours.

Serves 4-6.

Rice Casserole

1 lb. mild sausage, chopped	1 cup uncooked rice
1 cup chopped celery	1 cup water
1 onion, chopped	2 cans cream of mushroom soup
1 4 oz. canned mushroom, sliced	salt and pepper

Brown sausage. Remove fat. Saute celery and onion with sausage. Let cool. Add mushrooms, rice, water and soup. Add salt and pepper to taste. Bake in casserole dish at 300 degrees for 1 1/2 to 2 hours. Sliced or silvered almonds may be sprinkled as topping.

Quickie Salisbury Steak

1	can cream of mushroom soup	1	egg, slightly beaten
1 1/2	lb. hamburger	1/4	cup onion, finely chopped
1/2	cup dry bread crumbs	1/3	cup water

Mix 1/4 cup of cream of mushroom soup and remaining ingredients (except water); mix thoroughly. Shape into patties and place in a shallow baking dish. Bake 30 minutes at 350 degrees. Spoon off fat.

Mix remaining soup and water; pour over meat. Bake 10 minutes longer.

Teri Hamburger Meat Loaf

2	lb. hamburger	1/2	cup shoyu
4	slices bread	1/2	cup sugar
1/2	cup milk (optional)	1	clove garlic, minced
2	eggs	1	slice ginger, minced
1	onion, sliced	1/2	tsp. ajinomoto

Combine hamburger, bread, milk, eggs and onion. Combine shoyu, sugar, ginger, garlic and ajinomoto. Add to the hamburger mixture. Put in baking dish. Bake at 375 degrees for 45 minutes to 1 hour.

Hamburger with Tofu

4	Tbsp. shoyu	1	egg
3 1/2	Tbsp. sugar	1	lb. hamburger
	minced garlic		chopped round onion
	grated ginger	1/2	block tofu (mashed)

Mix shoyu, sugar, garlic, ginger and egg. Add hamburger, onion and tofu. Shape into patties and fry.

Braised Swiss Steak

Combine in a bowl:

6 Tbsp. flour	24 pieces cubed steak
3/4 tsp. salt	(4 oz. each)
1/2 tsp. paprika	salad oil (enough to
1/8 tsp. garlic powder	brown steak)
1/8 tsp. onion powder	

Dredge steaks in the flour mixture. Brown in hot oil, drain excess oil. Lay steaks in baking pan.

1 block margarine	1/2 lb. celery
1 medium onion	1 large green bell pepper
3/4 oz. carrot	

Julienne veggies, saute with margarine until tender. Sprinkle over steaks in pan.

Mix together until smooth:

1/4 cup plus 1 Tbsp. flour	1/4 tsp. black pepper
1 1/4 qt. water	1/2 tsp. garlic powder
1 1/2 cups ground tomatoes	1/2 tsp. onion powder
2 1/2 Tbsp. beef flavor base	1/2 tsp. Worcestershire sauce
3/4 tsp. salt	1/2 tsp. marjoram

Add tomato mixture to the rest of the ingredients. Bring to a boil, pour over steaks, and cover tightly with foil. Bake 350 degrees in oven for 45 minutes.

Roy's Asian Beef Lasagne

with Roasted Spicy Garlic
by Roy Yamaguchi

Scallion Oil:

1 cup olive oil	1 tsp. minced garlic
1 cup green onions	1 tsp. minced ginger

Slowly cook olive oil, green onions, garlic and ginger until the green onions are softened. Place oil in a blender and blend until smooth. Strain and reserve only oil.

Roasted Spicy Garlic (serves 4):

1 head of garlic	1/8 tsp. sugar
1/8 tsp. hichimi pepper	1 tsp. soy sauce
1 tsp. minced ginger	1 Tbsp. olive oil

Chop off a third of the top of a head of garlic and place in a saute pan. Sprinkle garlic with hichimi pepper, ginger, sugar, soy sauce and olive oil. Place garlic in oven at 400 degrees for 20 minutes.

Beef Marinade:

4 oz. julienne New York fillet of beef	1/8 tsp. black sesame seeds
1 Tbsp. chopped green onions	1/2 tsp. sugar
1/4 tsp. minced garlic	1 tsp. soy sauce
1/4 tsp. minced ginger	1 tsp. sesame oil

Combine all ingredients in a bowl and marinate.

Continued on next page.

Roy's Asian Beef Lasagne (continued from previous page)

Stir Fry:

1	Tbsp. canola oil	1/4	cup bean sprouts
1/4	cup julienne green bell peppers	1/2	cup chopped mustard cabbage
1/4	cup julienne red bell peppers	1/4	tsp. minced garlic
		1/4	tsp. minced ginger
1/4	cup julienne yellow bell peppers	1/8	tsp. black sesame seeds

In a hot saute pan add oil and stir fry beef, bell peppers, bean sprouts, mustard cabbage, garlic, ginger and black sesame seeds. Stir and toss for about 20 seconds.

Plate:
   6   gyoza wrappers (previously parboiled)
1/4   cup cilantro

Place a gyoza wrapper on a plate. Place one third of the beef & vegetable mixture on top and repeat the procedure 2 times (3 gyoza wrappers are needed for each serving). Remove 4 cloves of the baked garlic from the skin and place on top. Drizzle scallion oil over lasagne and garnish with cilantro. (serves 2)

BBQ Meatballs

1	lb. hamburger meat	2	Tbsp. vinegar
1/2	cup catsup	1	Tbsp. Worcestershire sauce
2	Tbsp. brown sugar	2	tsp. prepared mustard
1	Tbsp. shoyu		(hot dog)

Prepare hamburger as for patties, but shape into meatballs. Then cook meatballs, turn over, pour sauce and simmer till done.

Roast Corn Meal Crusted Pork Loin

Sweet Corn BBQ Sauce
by 3660 On the Rise

1	tsp. garlic	1	tsp. cumin
1	tbsp. chopped onion	1/4	tsp. cayenne
2	cup beef stock	1/2	cup fresh roasted corn
1	tbsp. mustard (Dijon)		(cut off cob)
1/2	cup ketchup	1	tsp. fresh chopped oregano
1	tsp. salt	1	Tbsp. fresh chopped cilantro

Lightly saute onion and garlic over medium high heat. Add the rest of the ingredients and simmer for about 10 minutes. Puree in blender, keep warm.

1	3-4 lbs. pork loin, boneless	1/4	cup vegetable oil
2	cups cornmeal		salt and pepper to taste

Salt and pepper the pork loin and roll in cornmeal. Heat skillet till hot. Add oil and sear porkloin on both sides. Preheat oven to 350 degrees. Roast porkloin for about 30 to 45 minutes.

Braised Pork Chops

4-6	pork chops	1	cup hot water
	salt		juice of 1/2 lemon
	pepper	1	onion (thinly sliced)
	garlic salt	2	medium sized potatoes
	flour		(thinly sliced)
3	cubes beef bouillon	2	Tbsp. parmesan cheese

Season pork chops with salt, pepper and garlic salt. Roll in flour and brown in a large skillet. Dissolve bouillon cubes in hot water and add lemon juice. Drain oil from skillet. Layer onions, potatoes and cheese over pork chops in skillet. Pour bouillon sauce all over, cover skillet and simmer for 45-60 minutes.

Rack of Lamb with French Lentil Ragout

For the ragout:

4-5	slices bacon	1	lb. lentils or French
1	onion		green lentils
1	carrot	1	qt. vegetable broth
3	ribs celery	1	tsp. thyme
10	shiitake mushroom caps	1	bay leaf
1	tsp. minced garlic		

For the lamb:

3 racks of lamb   Dijon mustard
Seasoned bread crumbs

Dice the bacon and cook in a heavy skillet to render its fat. Dice the onion, carrot, celery, mushrooms and garlic; add them to the bacon. Cook until the onions are translucent. Add the lentils, broth and herbs and bring to a simmer. Cook 20 to 30 minutes, or until the lentils are soft but not mushy. Season to taste and keep warm.

Sear the lamb racks in a skillet over high heat until browned all over. Let them cool. Spread them with a thin layer of Dijon mustard, then press the bread crumbs into the mustard and bake at 350° for 25 to 30 minutes for medium rare meat.

To serve, slice the lamb into double chops and arrange on the plate over the lentil ragout. Fresh long green beans compliment this dish well.
Serves 6 people.

Lamb in Puff Pastry

with Mint Pesto

1	cup fresh mint leaves	1	17 oz. package frozen
1	garlic clove		puff pastry, defrosted
1/4	cup olive oil	1	egg yolk, beaten
1/2	tsp. salt or to taste		fresh mint for garnish
12	loin chops, 1 inch thick		

Preheat the oven to 425 degrees. To make the pesto, place mint, garlic, oil and salt in the bowl of a food processor and puree. Cut the lamb tenderloins from the bones and trim all fat. Roll out the puff pastry into a rectangle 1/8 inch thick. Trim the edges so they are straight. Cut the pastry into 12 rectangles, each large enough to enclose a lamb medallion. Place 1 piece of lamb at the bottom half of each rectangle and top with a heaping tablespoon of pesto. Fold dough over to enclose the lamb, and crimp the edges tightly. Brush each package lightly with beaten egg and place on a baking sheet. Bake until the meat is done and the pastry is golden brown, about 10 minutes for rare meat, 15 minutes for medium rare. Garnish with mint leaves.

Serve this with new potatoes simply prepared, and for a vegetable, julienned sauteed zucchini or julienned honeyed carrots work well. This dish is very simple, but very elegant. Do not over cook the lamb. Medium rare seems to be best.

Makes 6 servings.

Oxtail Stew

Ox Tails
oil
garlic
1 large can V8 drink
water (fill 1/2 of V8 can)

1 pkg. Lipton Beefy
  Onion soup mix
2 carrots
3 potatoes
1 round onion

Flour oxtails and brown in oil and garlic. Add V8 drink, water and Lipton soup mix. Boil until tender. Add chopped carrots, potatoes and onion. Simmer until vegetables are cooked.

Lea's Delicious Rib Roast

3 ribs or larger roast
1/2 cup shoyu
1/2 cup flour
rock salt

coarse pepper
1 can chicken broth – optional
1 cube beef boullion – optional

Start in morning to prepare. Rub a small amount of rock salt and coarse pepper around entire roast. Mix flour and shoyu and rub/coat roast. Let beef stand at room temperature for 1 hour. Heat oven to 375 degrees and roast for 1 to 1 1/2 hours depending on the size of the roast. Turn off oven. Let stand in the oven without opening the oven door all day.

To serve: Reheat oven to 375 degrees and roast beef for 30 minutes for medium rare; or 40 minutes to 1 hour for well done. Ajus can be made with drippings or by heating 1 can chicken broth with 1 cube beef bullion.

Barbecue Ribs (Sesame Seed)

5 lbs. spare ribs
2-3 pieces ginger
3/4 cup sugar
1 cup catsup

3/4 cup shoyu
1/3 cup oyster sauce
ajinomoto
sesame seed

Boil ribs and ginger in water for 1 hour and drain. Combine remaining ingredients except sesame seeds and marinate ribs in sauce for 1 hour. Sprinkle sesame seeds and broil.

Baked Short Ribs

3 lbs. short ribs rolled in 1/2 cup flour
Lay on top ribs:
  1 large onion, sliced
  1 stalk celery, sliced (optional)

Sauce:

3/4	cup catsup	4	Tbsp. shoyu
2	Tbsp. vinegar	1/2	cup sugar
2	Tbsp. worcestershire sauce	3/4	cup water

Pour sauce mixture over ribs & cover with foil. Bake at 350 degrees for 2 1/2 to 3 hours. Remove excess oil and serve.

Peachy Spareribs

2-3	lbs. spareribs	2	tsp. salt
1/2	cup brown sugar	2	tsp. powdered ginger
1/2	cup ketchup	2	small jars of baby
2	Tbsp. shoyu		food peaches

Combine brown sugar, ketchup, shoyu, salt, ginger and peaches for sauce. Mix well. Line 9" x 13" pan with foil and put ribs in pan. Bake at 400 degrees for 30 minutes. Then pour drippings out. Pour sauce over ribs and bake approximately 1 hour at 325 degrees or until meat is soft.

Indich Spareribs

1	cup unflavored yogurt	1/2	tsp. chili powder
2	tsp. grated orange peel	1/2	tsp. ground cumin
1	tsp. grated lemon peel	3	cloves garlic
1/4	cup orange juice	1/4	cup packed Italian parsley
2	Tbsp. lemon juice	1/4	cup catsup
1	Tbsp. crushed dried hot red chilies (or to taste)	4	lbs. pork spareribs
		2	Tbsp. honey

Puree yogurt, orange peel, lemon peel, orange juice, lemon juice, chilies, chili powder, cumin, garlic, parsley and catsup. Marinate ribs in sauce for a minimum of 3 hours. Drain ribs reserving marinate. Mix reserved marinade with honey. Bake ribs at 400 degrees covered for 15 minutes. Uncover and baste every 15 minutes until ribs are very tender (about 1 hour).

Ham with Cherry Sauce

Ham

Sauce:

2	tsp. whole cloves	3	tsp. Coleman mustard
3	cup brown sugar	2	cans crushed pineapple
16-18	maraschino cherries	2	tsp. sherry
2	Tbsp. white vinegar		

Score ham and pierce cloves in ham. Mix rest of ingredients to make sauce. Baste ham in sauce. Bake ham at 350 degrees for 1 1/2 hours or 10 minutes for each pound. Baste with sauce every 10 minutes.

Baked Ham with a Guava Sherry Sauce

by 3660 On the Rise

1	Ham bone in and scored (stud with cloves, optional)	3	whole cloves
2	cups 7-Up	1/4	cup guava jelly
4	cups guava nectar or juice	1	juice of lemon
1/2	cup sweet sherry	3	Tbsp. cornstarch
1	cinnamon stick	4	Tbsp. water
			salt and pepper to taste

Baking:

Set studded ham in roasting pan and place in oven with temperature set at 375 degrees for about 10 minutes. Reduce temperature to 325 degrees. At this time combine 2 cups of 7-Up with one cup guava nectar. Baste generously with the mixture. Return ham back to oven. Baste every 15 minutes till mixture is done. Depending on the size of the ham, allow 10 minutes per pound. When mixture is done baste with the juices in the roasting pan.

Sauce:

Combine the balance of the guava juice, sherry, cinnamon stick, cloves, guava jelly, lemon juice and the drippings from the ham. Reduce till mixture is 3/4 of volume. Season and thicken with cornstarch and water. Strain and serve.

Note:

Fresh guavas can be substituted for the juice. To use fresh guavas, pare skin and blend pulp in blender till smooth. Strain through a sieve. Fresh guava juice is not as sweet as the prepared juice. More sugar, jelly, or honey can be added to sauce.

Chinese Style Baked Ham

3/4	cup brown sugar	2	Tbsp. hoisin sauce
1	small can crushed pineapple	1	ham
1/2	tsp. sesame oil		

Mix sauce ingredients together. Cook ham on low heat in covered pot. When ham is almost done, add sauce. Cook until done.

Pot Roast Pork

5	lbs. pork butt	1	cup water
1	clove garlic	1	cup chicken broth
1	inch ginger		carrots
1/3	cup sugar		potatoes
1/2	cup shoyu		onions
1/3	cup vinegar		

Brown pork butt with garlic and ginger. Add remaining ingredients, except vegetables. Simmer for 2 hours, turning the meat occasionally. Add vegetables and simmer until done. Thicken sauce with cornstarch if desired. Optional: May substitute chicken for pork butt.

Pork and Peas with Pimento

1	lb. pork, sliced thin	1	can (4 oz) tomato sauce
2	cloves garlic, minced		dash of MSG (optional)
1	tsp. salt	1	pkg. frozen peas
2	bay leaves	4	tsp. pimento, chopped
1/4	tsp. pepper		
1	medium onion, minced		

Saute pork and garlic until brown. Pour out excess oil and cook pork until done. Mix in salt, bay leaf, pepper, onions, MSG and tomato sauce. Simmer for 10 minutes. Add peas and simmer for 1 minute. Add pimento and serve.

VEGETARIAN DISHES & BREADS

Tofu Curry

	flour	1	Tbsp. curry powder
1-2	blocks tofu	1	cup water
2	Tbsp. oil	1/2	tsp. salt
1	large onion sliced	1/2	tsp. honey
4	tomatoes chopped	2	Tbsp. cornstarch
1	tsp. grated ginger	1	Tbsp. shoyu
1	clove garlic minced		

Slice tofu and coat with flour. Fry in 2 Tbsp. oil until light golden. Remove from skillet and set aside. In the same skillet, saute the onions. Add tomatoes, ginger, garlic, curry, water, salt and honey. Cook stirring for approximately 5 minutes or until the onion is soft. Mix cornstarch and shoyu together. Add to curry mixture. Stir. If mixture gets too thick, add water. Add tofu to the curry mixture and stir gently just to heat and serve.

Fried Tofu

1	block firm tofu – drain well	green onions – sliced
	flour	bonito flakes (optional)
	oil	

Cut tofu into 16 square pieces. Coat each piece with flour and fry in oil. Do not turn tofu too early or it will break apart. Fry until slightly brown and drain on a paper towel.

Sauce:

1	cup water	1/4	cup light shoyu or tamari
2	tsp. Bragg liquid amino	1/4	cup mirin

In a small sauce pan, combine all ingredients and bring to boil. Top tofu with green onions and bonito flakes. Pour hot sauce over tofu and serve warm.

Tofu Lasagne

1 pkg. wide lasagne noodles	1/2 cup grated fresh parmesan
1 qt. spaghetti sauce	cheese
8 oz. mozzarella cheese, sliced thin	

Filling:

2 cups tofu, drained and mashed	1 tsp. dried parsley
1 cup cottage cheese (small curd)	1/2 tsp. black pepper
	2 eggs (optional)

Prepare noodles according to package directions. Drain thoroughly. Set aside. While lasagne is cooking, prepare filling mixture by placing all the ingredients in a large bowl and mixing thoroughly. Set aside. To assemble the lasagne, layer the noodles across the bottom of an 8" x 12" pan. Spread a layer of filling over the noodles, then spread a layer of sauce over the filling. Lay slices of mozzarella over the sauce. Repeat layering. Top casserole by sprinkling parmesan cheese evenly over mozzarella cheese. Bake at 350° F for 50 minutes or until bubbly and golden brown. Serves 8 people.

Tofu Nori Salad

1 block tofu drained and cut in cubes	2 Tbsp. salad oil
1/4 cup sliced nori	2 Tbsp. shoyu
1 medium tomato	1 tsp. sesame oil
1 green onion chopped	

Combine above ingredients and chill.

Roy's Warm Tofu Salad with

Roasted Macadamia Nuts and Wilted Greens
by Roy Yamaguchi

Tofu:

Cut a 4 x 5 piece of firm tofu in four pieces about 1/2 inch thick.

Season with salt and hichimi pepper. Pour 1 Tbsp. macadamia nut oil over tofu and saute over high heat to a golden brown on both sides.

Stir Fry:

1/2 Tbsp. macadamia nut oil	1/2 cup fresh spinach (big leaves)
1 Tbsp. sesame oil	1/2 cup radicchio (big leaves)
1 tsp. minced ginger	1/2 cup watercress (with stem)
1 tsp. minced garlic	1/2 cup bean thread noodles
3/4 cup chopped mustard cabbage	(cooked, according to package directions)
1/2 cup chopped shiitake mushrooms	1 Tbsp. moromiso (Japanese soy bean condiment)
1/4 cup sugar snap peas	1 1/2 Tbsp. Thai fish sauce
1/3 cup bean sprouts	

In a hot wok add both oils. Add ginger and garlic and saute until brown. Stir fry mustard cabbage, shiitake mushrooms, sugar snap peas, bean sprouts, spinach, radicchio and watercress. Then add bean thread noodles, moromiso and fish sauce and stir for another 10 seconds.

Plate:

1/2 cup baby green or
1/2 cup of the stir fry vegetables
4 Tbsp. macadamia nuts, chopped

Place fried tofu on bottom of plate. Top with 1/2 cup baby greens and 1/2 cup of the stir fry vegetables. Finally, sprinkle chopped roasted macadamia nuts all over plate.

Serves 4 people.

Tofu Salad

Salad:

2	firm tofu (Nigari brand)
1	bag bean sprouts
2	cans boneless salmon (optional)
2	Maui onions (sliced)
1	bunch watercress
1	head cauliflower
1	bunch broccoli (par boiled)
6	medium tomatoes
1	bunch green onions

Sauce:

2	cup sugar
2	cup shoyu (Kikkoman)
4	cloves garlic (grated)
3	Tbsp. ginger (grated)
2	dash chili pepper (dried)
3	Tbsp. vegetable oil
3	Tbsp. sesame oil
1/3	cup white vinegar

Salad:

Cut tofu into cubes and line the bottom of serving pan or bowl. Cut bean sprouts into shorter lengths and spread over tofu. If using salmon, drain salmon and spread over bean sprouts. (Tuna may be substituted for salmon.) Slice onions and spread over salmon. Slice watercress into 2 inch lengths and spread over onions. Cut cauliflower into bite size pieces. Cut broccoli into bite size pieces, par boil, drain and cool before using. Spread cauliflower and broccoli over watercress. Dice tomatoes and spread over cauliflower and broccoli. Dice green onions and spread evenly over top.

Sauce:

Add sugar and shoyu into a pot. Grate garlic and ginger into sauce. (Garlic and ginger may be increased or decreased according to taste.) Add a couple of dashes of dried chili pepper or 1 fresh crushed chili pepper (remove crushed chili pepper before serving). Add vegetable oil and sesame seed oil to sauce. Add white vinegar. Taste sauce, if not tart enough add more vinegar to taste. (If too much vinegar was added just add more sugar to counteract the tartness.) Heat sauce till it boils then let cool before pouring over salad. Shake sauce vigorously to mix oil into shoyu mixture and pour over salad just before serving.

Easy Tofu Salad

1	block firm tofu	1	bunch watercress (use leafy
1	onion (sliced thin)		part, cut into 1 inch
1	tomato (sliced and		lengths)
	chopped big)		
1	can salmon (optional)		

Sauce:

1/2	cup olive oil	1/8	cup amino
3	cloves garlic (minced)	1/2	cup green onions
1/8	cup tamari (shoyu)		(sliced thin)

Layer: Tofu, salmon (if using), round onion, tomato, watercress.
Sauce: Heat oil with garlic (don't burn garlic) add tamari, amino and green onions (remove from heat). Pour over salad just before serving.

Hummus (Chickpea -Tahini Spread)

1	large onion, minced	1/2	cup fresh lemon juice
1-2	cloves minced garlic, to	1/4	cup tahini paste
	taste or 3 Tbsp. roasted garlic		salt, if desired to taste
1	Tbsp. vegetable oil	1	cup sour cream (optional)
2	cups cooked chickpeas		
	(garbanzo), drained and		
	rinsed if canned		

Saute onion and garlic in oil until soft and set aside. If using roasted garlic, mash garlic into puree and add to saute onion and mix well.

In a food processor, puree the chickpeas with the garlic onion mixture, lemon juice and tahini. Mixture will be thick. Season with salt, if desired.

Mix in the optional sour cream for a richer version.

Serve hummus with pita or crackers or as a dip for fresh vegetables. Makes 3 cups.

Hummus

2 cans (15 1/2 oz. size) garbanzo beans	2 cloves garlic, coarsely chopped
1/4 cup olive oil	pinch of cayenne pepper
1 Tbsp. white wine vinegar	salt to taste
1/4 cup coarsely chopped yellow onion	

Open both cans of garbanzos and drain the juice from one can. Pour the contents of both cans into a food processor or blender and add all other ingredients. Process until very smooth. Serve with pita bread, crackers, cucumber slices or any other kind of vegetables. For a thicker consistency, drain liquid from both cans.

Makes about 3-4 cups.

Frittatas

2 jars 6 oz. marinated artichoke hearts	1/4 cup fine dry bread crumbs
1 small onion, finely chopped	1/8 tsp. each pepper, oregano, tabasco
1 clove garlic, minced	2 Tbsp. minced parsley
4 eggs	2 cups shredded sharp cheddar cheese
1/4 tsp. salt	

Drain marinade from jars into frying pan. Chop artichokes. Saute artichokes, onion and garlic in frying pan until limp. Beat eggs with whisk, add crumbs, salt, pepper, oregano and seasonings. Stir in cheese and artichokes onion mixture. Pour into greased 7 x 11 baking pan. Bake at 325 degrees for 30 minutes. (Check from 20 minutes to prevent burning). Let cool and cut into 1 inch squares.

Zucchini Casserole

2 lbs. zucchini (about 4 large) sliced in large chunks. Boil 1 minute.
1 cup cooked rice (use left-overs)
1 cup mild cheddar cheese (grated)
1/2 cup round onion (minced)
1/3 cup olive oil
3 eggs, slightly beaten
1/4 tsp. tabasco sauce (optional)
1/4 tsp. rosemary
salt and pepper to taste

Mix all together. Pour into a greased casserole dish. Bake at 350 degrees for 40 minutes.

Veggie Burritos

by Sandee Norris - Crepe Fever and Mocha Java

The secret of these burritos is the bean sauce:

1 can Rosarita low fat vegetarian refried beans
2 cans undrained pinto beans
8 oz. tomato puree
1 diced onion
1 diced green pepper
4 cloves garlic crushed
1/2 tsp. cumin
1/2 tsp. cayenne
1 Tbsp. chili powder
1/2 tsp. black pepper (adjust spices to your own taste)

Mix all ingredients. Cook over med low heat, stirring frequently for about an hour, or until liquid is cooked down to desired consistency.

To make burritos:

Whole wheat tortilla (or chapati)

Spoon on beans, chunks of steamed red potatoes, onion, tomato, green pepper, and ripe olives. Roll up the burritos. Microwave for about 2 minutes. Serve with brown rice, lettuce on the side, garnish with salsa.

Vegetarian Chili

1 cup lentils	2 carrots, chopped
1 cup kidney beans (or 15 oz. can)	2 celery stalks, chopped
	2 8 oz. cans tomato sauce
1 cup garbanzo beans (or 15 oz. can)	1 can stewed tomatoes
	1 bay leaf
1 onion, chopped	1 Tbsp. chili powder
2 cloves garlic, minced	2 Tbsp. flour
3 Tbsp. olive oil	salt and pepper to taste
5-6 cups water	

Soak lentils according to package directions. Soak kidney and garbanzo beans separately. (If using canned beans, drain and set aside.) Saute onion and garlic in olive oil till transparent. Add water, carrots, celery, tomato sauce, stewed tomatoes, bay leaf and drained beans. Mix chili powder and flour together then add to above. Season with salt and pepper. Simmer for 1 hour.

Emma's Vegetarian Pizza

2 8 oz. Pillsbury Crescent roll mix
2 8 oz. cream cheese
1 pkg. Hidden Valley dressing
3/4 cup mayonnaise
   Chopped vegetables – broccoli, green pepper, red pepper, grated carrots, cauliflowers, olives and mushrooms

Spread crescent roll mix on 10" x 15" pan and bake at 350 degrees for 10-15 minutes. Blend together cream cheese, Hidden Valley dressing and mayonnaise and spread on cool dough. Sprinkle with chopped vegetables. Cover with saran wrap, and press down. Refrigerate. Cut in pieces.

Grilled Eggplant Salad

With Puna goat cheese, pesto and Mediterranean relish
by Chef Alan Wong of Alan Wong's Restaurant

2 pcs. round eggplant, sliced 1/2" thick	1 1/2 Tbsp. basil pesto
salt	2 Tbsp. Mediterranean Relish
olive oil	2 pcs. Ka'u orange, segments
4 pcs. vine ripened tomato, slices	2 pcs. chervil springs
	fresh bread croutons
1 oz. Puna goat cheese	1 Tbsp. basil oil
	1 tsp. aged balsamic vinegar

Season eggplant slices with salt. Allow eggplant to sweat, then marinate with olive oil. Grill eggplant over medium-high heat until fully cooked.

On plate, in a 2-1/2" diameter cylinder mold, layer ingredients starting with tomatoes, eggplant, goat cheese, basil pesto, 2nd layer of tomatoes, eggplant. Top off salad with Mediterranean relish. Garnish with oranges, chervil and croutons. Then remove mold. Drizzle basil oil and balsamic vinegar around salad.

Serves 1.

Mediterranean Relish

1 cup tomatoes, diced	4 anchovy fillets, diced
3 Tbsp. onion, diced	1 Tbsp. garlic, minced
1 Tbsp. capers	1 Tbsp. balsamic vinegar
1 Tbsp. basil	1 Tbsp. olive oil

Toss well in a bowl. Season with salt and pepper.
Yields 1-1/2 cups.

Continued on next page

Grilled Eggplant Salad (continued from previous page)

Basil Oil

2 oz. fresh basil sprigs	1/2 Tbsp. garlic, minced
1/2 oz. spinach leaves	2 Tbsp. water
1/2 pc. lemon	12 oz. olive oil
1 Tbsp. chili pepper water	salt and pepper to taste

Blanch basil and spinach, shock in ice water bath. In a blender, place all the above ingredients and puree until oil becomes bright green in color. Pass oil through a fine sieve to remove pulp.

Yields: 1 cup

Basil Pesto

6 anchovy fillets, diced	2 cups fresh basil
1/2 cup Macadamia nuts, chopped	1 Tbsp. garlic, minced
1/2 cup parmesan cheese, grated	4 oz. olive oil
1 cup spinach leaves	salt and pepper to taste

Place all ingredients into a blender. Puree until bright green.

Yields: 2 cups.

Chile Quiche

1	4 oz. can diced green chiles
1/2	lb. Monterey Jack cheese, grated
1/2	lb. sharp cheddar cheese, grated
2	eggs, beaten
4	Tbsp. flour
1/2	tsp. salt
1/3	cup milk

Mix ingredients together and put into a well greased 9" x 13" pan. Bake for 35 minutes at 350 degrees. Slice into squares when slightly cooled.

Monterey French Bread

1	loaf French bread
	butter
1	cup mayonnaise
1/2	cup parmesan cheese (grated)
1/2	cup chopped green onions
1	tsp. Worcestershire sauce

Mix together mayonnaise, parmesan cheese, green onions and Worcestershire sauce. Set aside. Cut French bread loaf in half (lengthwise) and slice almost through. Spread with butter and heat in oven. Remove from oven. Spread with mayonnaise mixture. Broil at 350 degrees until slightly browned.

Scones I

2	cups all-purpose flour	1/2	cup raisins
1/4	cup sugar	1	egg, beaten
2	tsp. baking powder	1	egg white, slightly beaten
1/2	tsp. salt (or less)		with fork
1/2	tsp. baking soda	1	tsp. sugar
1	block butter or margarine	1/8	tsp. cinnamon
1	cup buttermilk*		

In a bowl, pour hot water over raisins to cover. Let stand about 5 minutes, drain well and set aside. In large mixing bowl combine flour, sugar, baking powder, salt and baking soda. Cut in butter or margarine till mixture resembles coarse crumbs. Stir in raisins. In a small bowl blend buttermilk and egg (first beat eggs slightly with fork). Add this to crumb mixture and stir just until dough clings together. Knead about 10 strokes. Divide dough** into four 4 inch circles. Slice each circle completely through into quarters, but do not separate. Place on ungreased baking sheet. Brush with egg white. Combine sugar and cinnamon. Sprinkle sugar/cinnamon mixture over top. Bake in a 425 degree oven for 15 to 18 minutes, or till light brown. (Large circle may take a little longer to bake.)

* 1 cup milk plus 1 Tbsp. vinegar may be used instead of buttermilk.
** Dough may be divided into 2 or 3 circles, instead of 4.

Scones II

3 cups unsifted flour	1 cup buttermilk
6 Tbsp. sugar	1/2 cup currants
2 Tbsp. baking powder	egg whites
1/2 cup + 1 Tbsp. butter	

Sift first 3 ingredients together. Cut in butter. Stir in buttermilk and currants. Do not overbeat. Knead about 10 times. Divide dough into 2 equal parts. Roll dough to make a 6" circle (about 1" thick). With a knife, cut each circle into 6-8 wedges. Arrange each wedge on an ungreased baking sheet 1" apart. Brush tops with egg whites. Bake at 350 degrees for about 25 minutes.

Malasadas

1 pkg. dry yeast	1/2 cup sugar
1 tsp. sugar	1/4 cup melted butter
1/4 cup warm water	1 cup evaporated milk
6 eggs	1 cup water
6 cups flour	1 tsp. salt
1/4 tsp. lemon extract	

Dissolve yeast and the sugar in warm water. In small bowl beat eggs until thick. Put flour in large bowl, make well in center. Add yeast mix into eggs and add lemon extract, sugar, butter, milk, water and salt. Mix thoroughly to form a soft dough. Cover and let rise until double. In deep fat, drop dough by spoonfuls, fry until brown. Drain and roll in sugar.

Cornbread I

1/4 cup cornmeal	3 eggs, beaten
3 cups Bisquick	1 1/2 cup milk
1 cup sugar	3/4 cup butter or margarine,
3/4 tsp. baking soda	melted

Preheat oven to 350 degrees. Grease a 9" x 13" baking pan. In a large bowl, combine dry ingredients. Combine eggs and milk - stir into cornmeal mixture. Do not overbeat. Lightly stir in butter. Pour into prepared pan. Bake for 35 minutes or until done.

Corn Bread II

2 cups Bisquick	1 cup milk
5 Tbsp. cornmeal	2 eggs
1/2 tsp. baking powder	2 blocks butter, melted
3/4 cup sugar	

Mix all dry ingredients together in large bowl. Add milk and eggs. Mix. Add melted butter. Bake at 350 degrees in a 9" x 9" pan for 35 to 40 minutes.

Sour Cream Biscuits

4 cups Bisquick	1/2 tsp. baking soda
3/4 cup sugar	16 oz. sour cream
2 eggs	1 1/2 blocks butter, melted

Let sour cream stand out for about 20 minutes before starting. Mix the above ingredients (EXCEPT BUTTER) together. Spray PAM in 9" x 13" pan. Pour mixture in pan. Top with the melted butter. Bake at 350 degrees for about 20 to 25 minutes or until lightly browned.

Very Moist Banana Bread

1 cup butter	2 1/3 cups flour
2 cups sugar	2 tsp. baking soda
4 eggs	2 tsp. baking powder
3 cups mashed ripe bananas	1 tsp. salt
1/2 cup chopped nuts	1 tsp. cinnamon

Cream butter, sugar and add eggs one at a time. Fold bananas and nuts into cream mixture. Sift dry ingredients. Fold dry ingredients into banana mixture. Pour into greased and floured 13" x 9" pan. Bake at 325 degrees for 45 minutes.

Ono Banana Bread

1 cup margarine	2 1/2 cups flour
1 3/4 cup sugar	2 tsp. baking soda
3 large eggs, beaten	1/2 tsp. salt
5 large bananas, mashed	1/2 cup nuts

Cream together margarine and sugar. Mix eggs and bananas in separate bowl. Sift together flour, baking soda and salt. Alternately add a little banana mixture, then flour mixture to the creamed butter until all is added and mixed well. Add the nuts. Pour into greased and floured loaf pans.

Bake at 350 degrees for 45 minutes.

Sausage Bread

1	lb. Italian sausage	4	oz. mozzarella cheese
1	pkg. (10 oz.) frozen chopped spinach (thaw and squeeze out excess moisture)	2	loaves frozen Bridgeford bread dough

Remove sausage skin, cut into small pieces and saute sausage until well cooked. Add spinach to sausage and cook for about 3 minutes. Preheat oven to 400 degrees.

Roll dough flat to a 12" x 10" rectangle. Transfer to an oiled cookie sheet. Spoon sausage mixture evenly over half of the dough lengthwise, leaving 1/4" border. Cover with the cheese. Fold dough over filling and firmly press edges together. Brush the top with olive oil and sprinkle with pepper to taste. With a sharp knife make several slits on the top. Bake 15 to 20 minutes, until browned.

Pumpkin Walnut Bread

1 1/2	cups sugar	2	eggs, well beaten
1 2/3	cups all-purpose flour	1/2	cup vegetable oil
1/4	tsp. baking powder	1/2	cup water
1	tsp. baking soda	1	cup cooked mashed pumpkin
3/4	tsp. salt	1/2	cup coarsely chopped walnuts
1	tsp. cinnamon		butter for pans
1	tsp. cloves		flour for pans
1	tsp. nutmeg		

Preheat oven to 325 degrees. Mix all the dry ingredients in a large bowl. Add the eggs, oil, water, pumpkin and beat until well blended. Add the walnuts. Pour the batter into 2 buttered and floured 7" loaf pans. Bake for 50 to 60 minutes or until a toothpick inserted in the center comes out clean. Cool for 5 minutes in the pans then remove bread onto a rack.

This recipe can be doubled or tripled and can be frozen beautifully.

Pumpkin Bread

3 1/2 cups flour	1 tsp. nutmeg
1 tsp. salt	2 tsp. baking soda
3 cups sugar	1 tsp. allspice
1 tsp. cinnamon	1 tsp. baking powder

Mix all ingredients in large bowl and add the following to the above. Beat just until well blended. (DO NOT OVERBEAT)

4 eggs	2/3 cup water
1 cup Wesson oil	2 cups canned pumpkin
1 cup bleached golden raisins	

Add the following ingredients and fold this into batter quickly.
Bake in 4 medium loaf pans lined with waxed paper. Bake at 325 degrees for 1 hour.

King's Bakery Bread Pudding

1 loaf King's Bakery sweet bread	9 eggs beaten
1 1/2 blocks butter or margarine	raisins
1 cup sugar	cinnamon
3 cups milk	nutmeg
1 1/2 tsp. vanilla	

Melt butter, sugar and milk. Break bread into large pieces in greased 9" x 13" pan. Sprinkle raisins over bread pieces. Let melted butter mixture cool till warm. Add eggs (make sure mixture is not too hot or else it will curdle). Add vanilla and pour over bread (use a small cup to pour evenly over bread). Sprinkle top with cinnamon and nutmeg. Bake at 350 degrees for 20 to 25 minutes.

Banana Bread Pudding with Caramelized Banana Sauce

by "3660 On the Rise"

2	French bread sliced 1 to 1-1/2" thick	9	eggs
1 1/2	cups butter	1	1/2 qt. heavy cream
3	cups sugar	1	tsp. vanilla extract
		1/2	cup heavy cream

Cream butter and sugar till light and fluffy or until light in color. Add eggs in one at a time. Add heavy cream, vanilla extract and mix. Pour mixture over three layers of sliced French bread. Sprinkle each layer with cinnamon. Pour 1/2 cup of heavy cream over bread pudding. Let soak for about 30 to 45 minutes. Press bread down to ensure that the mixture is coating all of the bread. Cover pudding with aluminum foil and bake in oven in a water bath at 350 degrees for about 1 hour 15 minutes. Remove foil and bake uncovered for about 15 minutes.

Caramelized Banana Sauce:

1/4	lb. butter		dash cinnamon
1/4	lb. brown sugar	4	Tbsp. creme de banana liquor
1/2	lemon juice		sliced bananas

Caramelize butter and brown sugar in a sauce pan. Add lemon, cinnamon and creme de banana. Simmer for about 3 to 4 minutes till alcohol burns out. Add sliced bananas and simmer for about 2 minutes. Serve under or over bread pudding.

DESSERTS

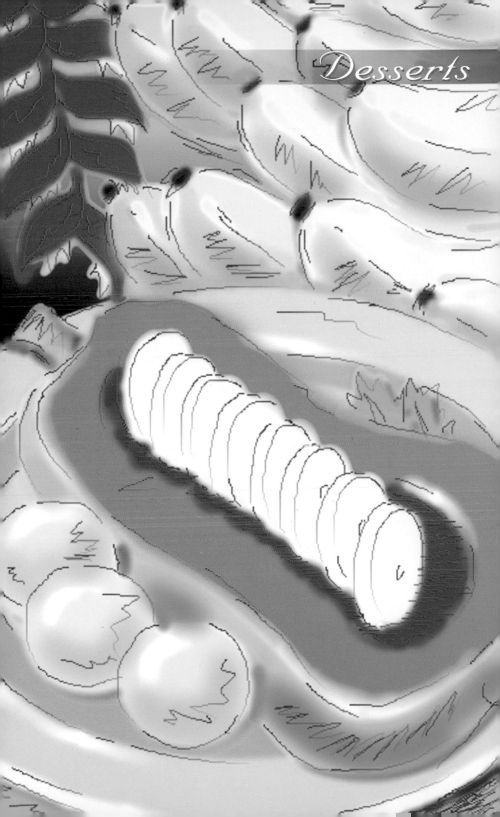

Double Chocolate Brownies

3/4 cup flour	12 oz. semi-sweet chocolate
1/4 tsp. baking soda	chips - divided
1/4 tsp. salt	1 tsp. vanilla extract
3/4 cup sugar	2 eggs
1/3 cup (5 1/3 Tbsp.) butter	1/2 cup chopped nuts (optional)
2 Tbsp. water	

Preheat oven to 325 degrees. Grease 9" square pan. In a small bowl, combine flour, baking soda and salt. Set aside. In small saucepan over medium heat, combine sugar, butter and water. Bring to a boil, stirring constantly, remove from heat. Add 1 cup chocolate chips and vanilla; stir until smooth. Transfer to a large bowl. Add eggs, one at a time, beating well. Gradually blend in flour mixture. Stir in remaining chocolate chips and nuts. Spread in prepared pan. Bake 28 to 33 minutes until just set. Cool completely.

Easy Sour Cream Muffins

1 8 oz. container sour cream
1/4 cup sugar
1 egg, beaten slightly
2 cups Bisquick, smash lumps
1/2 tsp. baking soda

Combine dry ingredients. Stir egg and sour cream together and mix to dry ingredients. Pour into greased or paper lined pans and bake at 325° for 15 to 20 minutes.

Low Fat Blueberry Muffins

1 egg (or use 1/4 cup cholesterol-free substitute such as Egg Beaters)	1/3 cup sugar
	1 Tbsp. margarine, melted
	3/4 cup fresh or frozen blueberries
1 3/4 cups reduced fat Bisquick	(thawed and drained)
3/4 cup skim milk	

Beat egg slightly in medium bowl. Stir in remaining ingredients except blueberries until just moistened. Fold blueberries into batter. Pour in lined muffin tins. Bake in 400 degree oven 13 to 18 minutes or until golden brown. Makes one dozen muffins.

Raisin Bran Muffins

2 1/2 cups sugar	1 qt. buttermilk
5 tsp. baking soda	1 cup vegetable oil
5 cups all-purpose flour	4 eggs, beaten
7 1/2 cups (15 oz. box) Post Natural Raisin Bran Cereal	cinnamon – optional
	sugar – optional

Blend sugar, baking soda and flour in large mixing bowl. Stir in cereal. Add buttermilk, oil and eggs and blend until dry ingredients are moistened. DO NOT STIR BATTER AGAIN. Fill lightly greased muffin pans 2/3 full. Bake at 400 degrees for 15-20 minutes.

If desired, lightly brush melted butter over batter and sprinkle with cinnamon and sugar before baking.

Date and Nut Squares

1/4   cup butter
3/4   cup sugar
 1   egg

1 2/3   cup Bisquick
 1   cup chopped dates
1/2   cup chopped nuts

Heat oven to 350°. Grease and flour 9"x9" pan. Mix butter, sugar and egg. Add Bisquick, dates and nuts. Spread in pan, bake until light brown (approx. 20-25 minutes). Cool, cut into 1 1/2" squares and roll in powdered sugar if desired.

Optional – you may substitute raisins for dates.

Very Ono Mandarin Orange Cake

Cake:

 1   box yellow cake mix - Duncan Hines Traditional
1/2   cup vegetable oil
 4   eggs
 1   can mandarin oranges (including liquid)

Mix all ingredients. Grease a 9" x 13" cake pan with vegetable shortening. Pour cake mix in pan. Bake for 35-40 minutes in 350 degree oven.

Frosting:

 1   can crushed pineapple or cut up peaches
 1   tub 8 oz. Cool Whip (defrosted)
 1   box instant vanilla pudding

Mix all together in a bowl. Frost cake. Refrigerate.

Poppy Seed Cake

1   box yellow cake mix
1   box instant vanilla pudding
4   eggs
1/2 cup Wesson oil

1   tsp. almond flavoring
1   cup hot water
4   Tbsp. poppy seeds

Mix together all ingredients. Bake in greased and floured bundt pan or 9" x 13" pan at 350 degrees for 30-35 minutes.

Chocolate Pudding Crust Cake

Crust:

2   blks. butter
2   cups flour
1/4 cup brown sugar

Mix and spread in pan.
Bake at 350 degrees for
15-20 minutes.

Filling:

8   oz. Philadelphia
     cream cheese (soft)
8   oz. Cool Whip
     (medium size)
1   cup powdered sugar

Blend. Spread on cooled crust.

Topping:

2   boxes instant chocolate pudding
1   box instant vanilla pudding
3   cups cold milk

Prepare pudding per box directions. Spread on filling. Refrigerate.

Banana Cream Squares

Crust:

1 1/2 blocks butter	3 Tbsp. powdered sugar, sifted
1 1/2 cups flour	3/4 cup nuts (optional)

Melt butter. Mix all ingredients in a 9" x 13" pan. Spread evenly and press. Bake for 15 minutes at 350 degrees. Cool when done.

Filling:

1 8 oz. cream cheese	6 large bananas
3 cups milk	Cool Whip
2 pkg. instant vanilla pudding	

Beat cream cheese, milk, and pudding for 3 minutes. Slice banana into 1/2 inch pieces. Spread bananas evenly on crust. Spread mixture over bananas. Refrigerate for at least one hour. Top with Cool Whip.

Banana Cupcakes

2 blks. margarine	2 1/2 cups flour
1 cup brown sugar	1 tsp. salt
3 large or 4 medium eggs	2 tsp. baking soda
3 cups mashed bananas	

Cream margarine and add sugar. Add one egg at a time. Add bananas. Sift together flour, salt and baking soda. Add to creamed mixture. Pour in lined muffin tins. Bake at 350 degrees for 30 minutes.

New York Cheesecake

Step 1:

1 1/2   cups Graham cracker crumbs
1/4   cup sugar
1/3   cup melted butter/margarine

Mix together and press into bottom of 9" springform pan. Bake at 375 degrees for 7 to 8 minutes.

Step 2:

3   8 oz. pkgs. Philadelphia cream cheese
5   large eggs
1   cup granulated sugar
1/2   tsp. vanilla flavoring

Mix together until well blended. Food processor is easiest, but an electric mixer works well. Should be very creamy when mixed. Pour into pan with graham cracker crust on bottom. While baking, prepare step 3 (topping)*. Bake at 350 degrees for 50 minutes. Remove from oven.
*Pour topping on cake and return to oven. Bake 5 more minutes. Remove from oven and cool completely before removing from pan. (Otherwise cake will crack in the middle).

Step 3 (topping):

1   pint sour cream (do not use imitation or light)
1/2   cup sugar
1   tsp. vanilla

Diced Apple Cake

2 cups sugar	2 tsp. cinnamon
2 blks. butter	1 tsp. vanilla
2 eggs	3 cups apples - diced
2 cups flour	1 cup chopped nuts
1 1/4 tsp. baking soda	

Cream sugar with butter. Add eggs. Sift dry ingredients and add to mixture. Add vanilla, apples and nuts. Bake at 325 degrees for 45 or more minutes in a 9" x 13" pan.

Easy Apple Cake

2 cups apples, peeled and sliced thinly.
1 slightly beaten egg
1/2 cup salad oil

Combine egg and salad oil, pour over apple slices until well coated; set aside.

1 cup sugar	1 tsp. baking soda
1 cup flour	1/2 tsp. cinnamon
1/2 tsp. salt	1/4 tsp. nutmeg

Sift dry ingredients together and add apple mixture to dry ingredients. Mix until moist. Pour into 8" x 8" x 2" baking pan. Bake at 350 degrees for 30 minutes.

Pineapple Upside Down Cake

1 pkg. yellow cake mix (Duncan Hines)	4 eggs
	1 cup water
1 pkg. instant vanilla pudding	1/2 cup oil

Put all ingredients in large bowl - beat until all ingredients are mixed.

Topping:

1 blk. butter	1 15 oz. can pineapple –
1/2 cup brown sugar	chunk, crushed or sliced

In 9" x 13" pan, melt butter and sugar. When butter is melted, mix so that there are no sugar lumps. Drain the pineapple and arrange on top of the butter mixture. Pour the cake mixture over and bake at 350 degrees for 35-40 minutes. When cake is done, cool for 10-15 minutes and turn cake over onto cookie sheet or larger platter.

Grandma's Prune Cake

1 cup butter	3 tsp. baking soda
1 1/2 cups sugar	1/2 tsp. cinnamon
4 eggs	1/2 tsp. cloves
1 cup cooked prunes (drained)	1 cup prune juice
2 1/3 cups cake flour	

Cream butter. Add sugar gradually, beat in eggs and add prunes. Sift flour, soda, cinnamon and cloves 3 times. Add prune juice alternately with flour mixture. Bake at 325 degrees for 25 minutes. Make 9" double layer cake.

Frosting:

3/4 cup sugar	2 eggs whites
1/3 cup water	

Boil sugar in the water (Do not mix). Beat egg whites. Add sugar mixture slowly to egg whites. Continue beating the mixture and egg whites. Frost cake.

Mango (Banana or Zucchini) Dream Cake

Cake:

1 box yellow cake mix
1/2 cup oil
4 eggs
1/2 cup water (1/4 cup water if using small/medium zucchini)
1 cup ripe mango (or banana or small/medium zucchini;
   if using large zucchini, discard center pulp and use 1/2 cup
   water), puree

Combine all and pour into 9" x 13" pan. Bake at 350 degrees for 30 minutes.

Topping:

1 8 oz. tub Cool Whip
1/3 cup milk
1 box instant vanilla (or banana cream) pudding
1 cup ripe mango or banana or 3/4 cup zucchini, puree

Combine and set in refrigerator. Pour on cooled cake and refrigerate one (1) hour before serving.

Carrot Pineapple Cake

3 eggs	1 cup walnuts
2 cups sugar	1 tsp. cinnamon
1 cup Mazola oil	1 tsp. vanilla
2 1/2 cups flour	2 cups grated carrots
1 tsp. salt	1 small can crushed pineapple

Beat eggs, sugar and oil. Add rest of ingredients and blend. Grease a 9" x 13" pan or 2 foil loaf pans. Bake at 350 degrees for 1 hour. Test to see if done.

Cracked Glass Jello Cream Cake

Crust:

1 1/2 cups flour	1/4 cup brown sugar
1/2 cup chopped nuts (optional)	
3/4 cup butter or margarine (block and a half)	

Mix together all ingredients and press into a 9" x 13" cake pan. Bake for 15 minutes at 350 degrees. Cool.

Jello:

1 pkg. (3 oz) strawberry jello	1 pkg. (3 oz.) lime jello
1 cup hot water	1 cup hot water
1 pkg. gelatin	1 pkg. gelatin
1 cup cold water	1 cup cold water

Mix together first 3 ingredients. Add cold water. Refrigerate in 8" x 8" pan until firm. Repeat above for lime jello. After both jellos are firm, dice jello and set aside in refrigerator.

Cream Cheese Mixture

1 blk. (8 oz) cream cheese	1 pkg. Dream Whip (follow instructions for 2 cups whipped cream)
1/2 cup sugar	
1 box (3 oz) lemon jello	
2 pkgs. gelatin	1/2 cup milk
1 cup hot water	1/2 tsp. vanilla
1 cup cold water	

Mix cream cheese and sugar until well-blended. Mix jello and gelatin. Add hot water and mix until well-blended. Add cold water to jello mixture and set aside to cool. Whip Dream Whip with milk and vanilla in mixer per instructions on package until peaks are formed. Add jello mix to cream cheese mixture, then fold in whipped cream.

Mix diced jello with cream cheese mixture and pour on top of cooled crust. Refrigerate overnight and cut into squares. Makes approximately 35 squares.

Rich Chocolate Rum Cake

1   box instant Duncan Hines
      Chocolate cake mix
4   oz. instant chocolate pudding
3   eggs (room temperature)

1/2   cup Mazola oil
1/3   cup Myers Dark rum
1   cup water

Mix all ingredients and bake in a bundt pan at 350 degrees for 1 hour. (This cake may be kept in refrigerator for months, but is usually eaten before that!)

Sour Cream Pound Cake

1   box Duncan Hines Golden
      Batter cake mix
1/3   cup sugar
1   blk. butter (melt and cool)

1   cup (8 oz.) sour cream
4   eggs
1/3   cup oil
1   tsp. vanilla

Mix all ingredients in a bowl with an electric beater. Bake in a 9" x 13" pan at 350 degrees for 40-45 minutes.

San Quentin Cake

2   cups chopped apples
1   egg
3/4   cup sugar
1/2   cup vegetable oil
1   cup flour

1/2   tsp. baking soda
1/2   tsp. salt
1/2   tsp. cinnamon
1/2   cup raisins
1/2   cup chopped nuts

Place in bowl all ingredients in given order and mix well. Pour into a lined 8" x 8" pan. Bake for 50-60 minutes at 350 degrees.

Pumpkin Cream Pie

Crust:

2 blks. margarine or butter
1/4 cup white sugar

2 cups flour

Mix and press into 9" x 13" pan. Bake at 350 degrees for 20 minutes or until golden brown.

Filling:

3 cups cold milk
3 pkgs. Jello vanilla flavor
   instant pudding
   (4 serving size)

1 1/2 cups canned pumpkin
1 1/2 tsp. pumpkin pie spice
1 cup thawed Cool Whip
   chopped nuts (optional)

Combine milk, pudding, pumpkin, spice and whipped topping in a deep bowl. Beat at lowest speed of electric mixer for 1-2 minutes. Pour into crust. Chill until set, at least 3 hours. Garnish with additional whipped topping and chopped nuts, if desired.

Pumpkin Praline Pie

by "3660 On the Rise"

1 unbaked pie shell
2 eggs
3/4 cup sugar
1/2 tsp. salt

1 tsp. ground cinnamon
1/2 tsp. ginger
2 cups pumpkin pie filling
1 2/3 cups evaporated milk

Mix all ingredients together and pour into pie shell. Bake for about 30 minutes or till center is set. Temperature should be at 350 degrees.

Praline Topping

1/3 cup sugar
1/3 cup brown sugar

3 Tbsp. half and half cream
1/2 cup chopped pecans

Mix all ingredients together and top pumpkin pie when it is almost done in the oven.

Chocolate Macadamia Nut Brittle Flan

by Ed Morris - Hawaii Prince Hotel

1/2 lb. sugar	1/2 tsp. cinnamon
1 lb. margarine	1/4 tsp. lemon extract
1 1/2 lbs. all purpose flour	1/4 tsp. vanilla extract
2 oz. egg whites	

Lightly mix together sugar and margarine. Combine sifted flour. Add remaining ingredients. Do not over mix. Roll out chilled dough and place in two 9" pie shells. Bake at 400 degrees until golden brown.

Brittle Filling

1 1/2 cups sugar	5 1/2 oz. butter
2 Tbsp. light corn syrup	1/2 cup cream
water	1 cup macadamia nuts

Combine sugar, light corn syrup and enough water to make a wet sand consistency. Boil until sugar carmalizes and turns a medium amber color. Add butter and mix thoroughly. Turn off heat, add cream slowly; be careful as it will splatter if too much is added at one time. Add nuts. Pour into pre-baked shells that are brushed with chocolate and refrigerate until cool.

Chocolate Topping

1 cup cream	4 egg yolks
1 Tbsp. cornstarch	6 oz. semi-sweet chocolate
1 cup sour cream	whip cream
2 eggs	chocolate shavings

Combine cream and cornstarch and mix well. Add all ingredients except semi- sweet chocolate in sauce pan over medium heat, stirring constantly. Let thicken, but do not boil. Remove pan from heat and add semi-sweet chocolate. Combine until melted. Pour over brittle layer then let set. Cover with whip cream and garnish with chocolate shavings.

Sour Cream Apple Pie

with Streusel Topping

3/4 cup sugar	1/4 tsp. nutmeg
2 Tbsp. flour	1 20 oz. can sliced apples,
dash salt	partially drained (apple
1 cup sour cream	pie filling may be used as
1 egg	a substitute)
1 tsp. vanilla	1 unbaked 9" deep dish pie shell

Streusel topping:

1/3 cup sugar	1/4 cup butter or margarine,
1/3 cup flour	cut into small pieces
1 tsp. cinnamon	

Preheat oven to 400 degrees. Sift sugar, flour and salt into bowl. Add sour cream, egg, vanilla and nutmeg. Beat until smooth. Stir in apples. Pour mixture into pie shell. Bake 15 minutes. Reduce temperature to 350 degrees. Continue baking until set.

For topping: Combine ingredients in bowl. Sprinkle evenly over pie Increase oven temperature to 400 degrees. Bake until top is browned, about 10 minutes.

Cool slightly before serving. Serves 8 - 10 people.

Custard Pie

3 eggs	1 tsp. vanilla
1/2 cup sugar	dash of nutmeg
1/4 tsp. salt	1 unbaked pie shell
2 1/4 cups milk, scalded	

Beat eggs slightly; add sugar, and salt gradually. Add heated milk and vanilla, beating constantly. Pour mixture into unbaked pie shell. Sprinkle with nutmeg.

Bake at 400 degrees for 15 minutes; then lower temperature to 350 degrees for 30 minutes.

Colorado Peach Cream Pie

1/2 cup sugar
  3 Tbsp. quick cook tapioca
1/2 tsp. vanilla
1/4 tsp. ground nutmeg
1/2 cup whipping cream
  1 Unbaked pastry for
       single-crust 9" pie

  6 cups peeled and sliced fresh
       firm ripe peaches (frozen
       peaches may be used if
       fresh not available)

In a small bowl combine sugar and tapioca. Mix in vanilla, nutmeg and cream. Let stand 15 minutes for tapioca to soften.

Pour peaches into pastry, then pour cream mixture evenly over fruit. Set pie in a foil lined 10" x 15" pan. Bake at 375 degrees on lowest rack until filling is bubbly and lightly browned and pastry is golden brown, about 45 to 50 minutes.

Lemon Cheese Pie

Shortbread crust:

  2 blks. butter
  2 Tbsp. powdered sugar

  2 cups flour
1/2 cup chopped nuts

Cream butter and add powdered sugar. Mix in flour and add chopped nuts. Press into a 9" x 13" cake pan and chill for 30 minutes. Bake at 350 degrees until lightly browned.

Filling:

  1 cup sugar
1/4 cup cornstarch
  1 cup water
  1 tsp. grated lemon peel

1/3 cup lemon juice
  2 egg yolks, beaten
  4 oz. cream cheese, softened

Combine sugar with cornstarch. Stir in water, lemon peel, lemon juice and egg yolks. Cook over medium heat, stirring until thick. Remove from heat and blend in softened cream cheese. Cool and pour into cooled crust. Chill.

Mango Cream Cheese Pie

Crust:
2   cup sifted flour

1/2   cup powdered sugar

1 1/2   blks. butter

Mix flour and powdered sugar. Cut in butter. Press into 9" x 13" pan. Bake at 350 degrees for 20 to 25 minutes. Cool crust.

Second layer:
1   8 oz. cream cheese

1/2   cup sugar

1   tsp. vanilla

1   8 oz. cool whip

Cream the cheese and sugar together. Add vanilla. Fold in cool whip. Spread over cooled crust and chill until firm.

Top layer:
2   envelopes unflavored gelatin

1   cup cold water

1   cup boiling water

4   Tbsp. lemon juice

1   cup sugar

5   cups mango (cut in 1/2" cubes)

Sprinkle gelatin over cold water. Add boiling water, lemon juice, and sugar. Mix well. Add mango to cooked gelatin. Chill till slightly firm. Pour over cheese layer. Refrigerate till serving.

Banana Cream Pie

Crust:

2 blks. butter	2 cups flour
2 Tbsp. sugar	sliced bananas

Mix butter, sugar and flour, pat in 13" x 9" pan; bake at 325 degrees for 20-30 minutes until brown; cool; line with bananas.

Filling:

1 8 oz. cream cheese	2 3 oz. pkgs. instant vanilla
3 cups cold milk	pudding

Cream cheese; beat with milk; add pudding. Pour over bananas. Refrigerate.

Topping:

1 8 oz. Cool Whip

Spread on top of pudding mix.

Apple Crisp

5 apples, peeled and sliced
sugar and cinnamon (optional)

Topping:

1 blk. butter/margarine, softened	3/4 cup oatmeal
	1/2 cup flour
3/4 cup brown sugar	1 tsp. cinnamon

Preheat oven to 350 degrees. Place apple slices in greased pan. If desired, sprinkle apple slices with sugar and cinnamon. Prebake apples for about 15 minutes or so, depending upon how tender you want apples. While apples are baking, prepare topping by combining all ingredients and mixing well until blended and crumbly. Remove apples from oven and evenly coat with topping mixture. Bake for another 30 minutes. Serve warm with milk or ice cream.

Ohelo Berry Cream Cheese Pie

Crust:

2 cups flour   2 blks. margarine
2 Tbsp. sugar

Cream Cheese Mixture:

8 oz. cream cheese   8 oz. Cool Whip
1 cup sugar

Topping:

3 cups Ohelo berries (cleaned)   1/4 cup cornstarch
3 cups water   2 3 oz. boxes of strawberry
1 cup sugar   Jell-O
1 tsp. salt   1 pkg. Knox gelatin

To prepare crust, cut margarine into flour and sugar. Press into 9" x 13" pan. Bake at 350 degrees for 25 minutes or until golden brown. Cool. Cream cup of sugar and cream cheese. Add Cool Whip and blend well. Spoon into the cooled crust. Cook berries in 1 1/2 cups water, sugar and salt until soft. Dissolve cornstarch in 1 1/2 cups water. Combine Jell O, gelatin and 6 Tbsp. water. Add dissolved cornstarch to slightly boiling berry mixture. Stir continuously until mixture thickens. Spoon some of the hot mixture into Jell-O mixture to soften. Pour Jell-O mixture into pot with berry mixture. Stir well and set aside to cool. When cooled, layer over cream cheese mixture and refrigerate.

Fresh Fruit Tart

by "3660 On the Rise"

Tart Dough:

4	oz. sugar		vanilla
8	oz. butter		dash of salt
1	egg	12	oz. all purpose flour

Mix together in a mixing bowl using a paddle all the ingredients except the flour. Add flour and mix till crumbly (small balls). Press dough into tart pans.

Chocolate Ganache:

2	Tbsp. heavy cream	1/3	cup chocolate chips

Heat the cream and add the chocolate chips and whisk till smooth. Reserve in a warm area.

Pastry Cream:

2	cups milk	3	egg yolks
1/2	cup sugar	1	Tbsp. butter
1/4	cup cornstarch		vanilla to taste

In a stainless steel pot add milk, sugar, cornstarch and egg yolks and cook slowly over low heat until the cornstarch taste is cooked out. Add butter and vanilla extract to taste.

Assembly of Fruit Tart

Bake tart shells in oven 325 degrees for 15 to 25 minutes till golden brown. Cool. Brush tart with chocolate ganache. Pour pastry cream into crust to the top of the crust. Cool. Place assorted fruits on top. Glaze with apricot glaze and refrigerate to set.

Peach Crisp Shortbread

Deep 9" x 13" pan - lightly sprayed with PAM

Crust:

1 cup sugar	1 1/2 cups butter or oleo
4 cups all-purpose flour	

Mix sugar and flour together. Cut butter or oleo into flour mixture using a pastry blender, until mixture looks crumbly. Press half of mixture into pan. Set aside.

Filling:

2 cans (28 oz. size) sliced peaches - well drained (overnight is best)	1/2 tsp. salt
	3 Tbsp. plus 1 tsp. flour (level)
1 can (1 lb. 5 oz. size) peach pie filling	1 Tbsp. cornstarch (level)
3/4 cup golden brown sugar - packed	1/4 tsp. cinnamon

Mix filling ingredients in a large bowl. Pour into bottom crust and level evenly. Sprinkle remaining crust over peach mixture.

Bake at 375 degrees for 35-40 minutes or until done.

Pineapple Cream Cheese Dessert

1 blk. butter or margarine	1 cup sifted flour
1/4 cup sugar	1/8 tsp. salt

Cut butter or margarine into sugar, flour and salt mixture. Press into 9" x 9" pan. Bake in 350 degrees oven for 10 minutes. Cool.

Cream:

1 8 oz. block cream cheese (softened)	1 cup fresh milk
1 tsp. vanilla	1 10 oz. can crushed pineapple
1 box vanilla instant pudding	Cool Whip

Combine cheese and vanilla; add instant pudding and milk gradually beating well. Add pineapple; pour into cooled crust. Refrigerate. Top with Cool Whip.

Snickerdoodles

2 1/2 cups all-purpose flour	1 cup shortening
2 tsp. cream of tartar	1 1/2 cups sugar
2 tsp. baking soda	2 eggs
1/2 tsp. salt	

Sift together flour, cream of tartar, baking soda and salt. Set aside.

Mix together and set aside:

1 tsp. cinnamon	2 tsp. sugar

Cream shortening and sugar until very fluffy. Add eggs one at a time, beating well after each addition. Gradually add dry ingredients, mix well. Form dough into walnut size balls, roll into cinnamon/sugar mixture.

Lay on PAM sprayed cookie sheet and press down lightly to flatten.

Bake at 350 degrees for 8 to 10 minutes. Cool on sheet for 3 minutes, take out and cool thoroughly on rack.

World's Best Peanut Butter Cookies

1 cup margarine or butter	2 cups flour
1 cup peanut butter	1 tsp. baking soda
1 cup sugar	1 6 oz. pkg semi-sweet
1 cup packed brown sugar	chocolate pieces
2 eggs	1/2 cup chopped roasted peanuts

Cream margarine and peanut butter. Gradually add sugar until blended. Add eggs, one at a time while beating until smooth. Sift flour. Add baking soda to flour and creamed mixture. Stir in chocolate and peanuts. Drop by teaspoonful onto greased baking sheets and flatten slightly using back of spoon. Bake at 350 degrees for 15 to 20 minutes. Makes 6 to 7 dozen.

Tophats

2 8 oz. cream cheese	12 oz. Cool Whip
3/4 cup sugar	30 foil-lined cups
2 eggs	30 Oreo cookies
1 tsp. vanilla	30 Mini Oreos (can substitute
2 pkgs. instant chocolate	with regular size Oreo
pudding	cookies cut into fourths)
2 1/2 cups milk	

Filling:

Mix together cream cheese, sugar, eggs and vanilla. Set aside.

Topping:

Mix together instant chocolate pudding and milk until thickened. Fold in 4 oz. of Cool Whip. Set aside.

Place 1 Oreo cookie into bottom of foil lined cups. Place cream cheese mixture over Oreos (about 1 Tbsp.). Bake at 350 degrees for about 15 minutes or until set. Cool. Top with pudding mixture and additional Cool Whip. When ready to serve, top with Mini Oreos.

Microwave Mochi

2 cups mochiko flour
1 cup sugar
2 cups water
1/4 tsp. vanilla

1/8 tsp. food coloring
      (red or green)
      potato starch

Mix all ingredients together till blended smooth. Pour into microwave tube pan that has been sprayed with PAM. Wrap in Saran wrap. Cook on high in microwave for 10 minutes. Cool completely. Place onto platter covered with potato starch. Cut into desired pieces.

Strawberry Mochi

3 cups water
1 cup sugar
1 box mochiko

1 can Koshian
    fresh strawberries
    potato starch (Katakuriko)

Wrap strawberries with Koshian and set aside for mochi wrap.
Boil water and sugar. Add mochiko a little at a time and mix well. Remove from heat. Place on a surface powdered with Katakuriko and pound well. Pull into small pieces and wrap strawberry and squeeze ends.
Makes 15 mochi pieces.

Cocoa Mochi

2 cups mochiko
1 3/4 cups sugar
3 Tbsp. ground cocoa
1 Tbsp. baking soda
1 can (12 oz) evaporated milk
2 eggs

1 can (12 oz) frozen coconut
    milk, thawed
1/4 cup butter or margarine,
    melted
1 tsp. vanilla

Set oven to 350 degrees. Grease a 13" x 9" x 2" pan. In a large bowl combine all ingredients and mix well. Bake for 1 hour. Cool before cutting. Makes 24 servings.

Coconut Mochi

1 box mochiko
2 1/2 cups sugar
2 cups water
1 can frozen coconut milk

1 tsp. baking powder
1 tsp. vanilla
    food coloring
    potato starch (Katakuriko)

Mix mochiko, sugar and water. Add rest of ingredients except potato starch and add food coloring of your choice (usually red, a few drops at a time). Pour into a greased 9" x 13" pan. Cover with foil and bake for 1 hour at 350 degrees. Cool for 30 minutes. Cut into desired pieces and roll in potato starch (Katakuriko).

Azuki Nantu

2 pkgs. mochiko (4 cups)	1 can Tsubushi Azuki
2 cups light brown sugar	2 1/2 cups milk or water
1 tsp. baking soda	1 12 oz. can coconut milk (frozen)

Mix everything together and pour into greased 9" x 13" pan. Bake for 1 hour at 350 degrees. Let cool then cut with plastic knife into pieces.

Manju

1 blk. butter	5 cups flour
1 blk. margarine	6 tsp. double acting baking
2 cups sugar	powder
4 eggs	1 can Koshian
1 tsp. vanilla	cream
1/4 tsp. yellow food coloring	

Cream butter, margarine and sugar. Add eggs, one at a time. Add vanilla and food coloring. Sift flour and baking powder. Add to the creamed mixture. Leave in refrigerator about an hour. Make into balls and flatten. Fill with "Koshian" and pinch together to seal. Brush top of manju with cream.
Bake at 350 degrees for 20 to 25 minutes or until nicely browned.

Strawberry Yokan

4 cups hot water	1 can Koshian
2 boxes Jello (strawberry, raspberry or cherry)	1 can Tsubushian
3 pkgs. Knox gelatin	

Add hot water to Jello and Knox gelatin and mix until dissolved. Add Koshian and Tsubushian and mix well. Pour into 9" x 13" pan. Cool, then refrigerate overnight.

Raspberry Koshian Jello

2   3 oz. boxes raspberry jello
2   3 oz. boxes mixed fruit jello
1   packet gelatin

4   cups boiling water
1   can 18 oz. koshian

Spray 9" x 13" pan with PAM. Mix jello and gelatin in large bowl. Add boiling water. Mix until jello is dissolved. Add koshian and mix well. Pour into pan and refrigerate.

Coffee Kanten

3   cups water
2   Tbsp. sugar
3   Tbsp. instant coffee
1   can Eagle sweetened condensed milk (14 oz)
4   pkgs. gelatin with 1 cup water

Heat water with sugar and instant coffee. Take off heat and add milk and gelatin mixture. Mix well. Pour mixture into 9" x 9" or 10" x 10" oil pan. Refrigerate and cut.

Goodie Goodie

2   cans strawberry soda
1   can condensed milk

1   can 7-Up

Mix all ingredients. Freeze for 3 hours. Whisk mixture and refreeze.

Haupia

4 lbs. grated coconut	1 box corn starch
6 qts. water	(Kingsford Brand)
1 3/4 cups sugar	2 1/2 cups water

Yield: Four 8" x 12" trays

Heat 4 lbs. grated coconut with 6 qts. of water. Bring to a boil. Cool and squeeze coconut juice in cheese cloth to yield 6 qts. of coconut milk. Prepare double boiler. In a small pot, blend 1 box corn starch with 2 1/2 cups water. In a large pot, pour coconut milk, sugar and blended corn starch, stirring constantly with a wire whisk as double boiler water comes to a boil. Stir with wire whisk constantly to bring coconut milk mixture to a smooth gel consistency. Pour into 8" x 12" trays. Refrigerate overnight.

Lemon Bars

Crust:

1 cup butter	2 cups flour
1/2 cup powdered sugar	

Mix and press onto the bottom of greased 9" x 13" baking pan. Bake at 350 degrees for 20 minutes.

Filling:

4 eggs	5 Tbsp. flour
6 Tbsp. lemon juice	1 tsp. baking powder
1 3/4 cups sugar	powdered sugar

Beat all ingredients well and pour onto crust. Bake at 300 degrees for 30 minutes. When warm, cut into bars. Sprinkle with powdered sugar when cool.

Texas Pecan Bars

Crust:

1 1/3 cups flour	1/4 tsp. baking powder
1/2 cup brown sugar (packed)	1/3 cup butter (softened)

Topping:

1 cup corn syrup	3 eggs
1 cup brown sugar	1 tsp. vanilla
1 Tbsp. flour	1 cup chopped pecans
1/2 tsp. salt	

Combine ingredients for crust and blend with mixer until particles are fine. Press into a greased and floured 9" x 13" pan. Bake at 350 degrees for 10 minutes. Combine ingredients for topping and pour over crust. Return pan to oven for 25 to 30 minutes. Cut when cool.

Granola Mix

4 cups uncooked oats	1/2 cup sunflower seeds
1/2 cup wheat germ	(may add more)
1/2 cup flaked coconut	1 tsp. ground cinnamon
1/2 cup sesame seeds	1 cup chopped almonds

Combine all of the above ingredients in large bowl and set aside.

1 cup honey	1 tsp. vanilla
1/2 cup chunky peanut butter	1 cup chopped dates
1/3 cup vegetable oil	1 cup raisins

Heat honey, peanut butter, vegetable oil and vanilla. Stir until smooth. Pour over dry mixture. Stir and spread in pan. Bake at 350 degrees for approximately 20 to 25 minutes. Stir occasionally while in oven. Add dates and raisins the last 10 minutes of baking.

Mom's Granola Bars

1	cup brown sugar (firmly packed)	1/2	tsp. baking powder
1/4	margarine or butter	1	cup oats
1	Tbsp. honey	1	cup Rice Krispies
1	egg white	1	cup raisins
1	cup flour	1/2	cup sunflower seeds (raw, unsalted)
1 1/4	tsp. cinnamon		

Preheat oven to 350 degrees. Grease 9" x 13" pan. Beat brown sugar, margarine, honey and egg white until well blended. Combine flour, cinnamon and baking powder and mix well. Mix flour mixture into margarine mixture. Stir in oats, cereal, raisins and sunflower seeds. Mix well. Firmly press mixture into bottom of pan. Bake for 14-20 minutes until brown. Cool completely and cut into bars. Yields 36 bars.

Lemon Cheese Bars

1	Duncan Hines pudding cake mix (yellow)	1	8 oz. Philadelphia cream cheese (soft)
2	eggs	1/3	cup sugar
1/3	cup oil	1	tsp. lemon juice

Mix dry cake mix with 1 egg and oil until crumbly. Reserve 1 cup of mixture. Pat remaining mixture lightly in ungreased 9" x 13" pan. Bake at 350 degrees for 15 minutes. Beat cheese, sugar, lemon juice and 1 egg until light and smooth. Spread over baked layer. Sprinkle 1 cup of reserved mixture over second layer. Bake at 350 degrees for 15 minutes. Cool.

Congo Bars

1 1/2 blks. butter
    Cream together.

1 box brown sugar (light)

3 eggs
    Add one at a time.

2 3/4 cup flour
    1 pkg (12 oz.) chocolate chips

3/4 tsp. baking powder
1 cup chopped walnuts
    (optional)

Add to above mixture. Bake in greased 8" x 8" and 13" x 9" pans at 325 degrees for 30 minutes.

Jello Cream Cheese

Crust:

2 blks. butter
2 cups flour

2 Tbsp. sugar

Mix; pat in 13" x 9" pan; bake at 325 degrees for 20-30 minutes until brown; cool.

Filling:

1 3 oz. box lemon jello
    Dissolve together; cool.

1 cup hot water

3/4 cup sugar
    Cream together.

1 8 oz. cream cheese

1 pkg. Dream Whip

Follow directions on box, whip; add to cream cheese mixture; add cooled lemon jello; stir and spoon over cooled crust; refrigerate.

Furikake Chex

1/4 cup shoyu + water to equal 1/3 cup	12 drops Tabasco
2/3 cup sugar	1 box Rice Chex
	2 pkgs. Nori Goma Furikake

Mix shoyu, sugar and tabasco together. Drizzle over Chex. Mix and sprinkle furikake over Chex. Bake at 250 degrees for 1 hour 10 minutes. Stir every 10 minutes to prevent sticking.

Brandied Peaches

3 or 4 ripe peaches	2 Tbsp. brown sugar
2 Tbsp. butter	brandy to taste

Have ready 2 quarts boiling water. Lower peaches into boiling water. Leave about 30 seconds then remove. Peel skin off peach. Heat butter in saute pan till bubbly, add brown sugar and mix well. Add peach slices and saute for 2 to 3 minutes. Add brandy and continue cooking for 2 to 3 minutes. Can be served immediately or refrigerated for up to two days. Serve over ice cream, sponge cake or in puff pastry shells.

Fresh Oranges with Grand Marnier

Makes a refreshing and simple dessert, great after a rich meal!

6 oranges	3 Tbsp. sugar or to taste (omit if oranges are sweet)
3 Tbsp. Grand Marnier, or to taste	Mint leaves, optional for garnish

Peel oranges, cutting away all traces of white pith. Slice oranges into bite size pieces discarding tough center core.

Season oranges with Grand Marnier and sugar. Garnish with mint leaves. Chill 2 hours and serve.

Notes

Index

Appetizers/Pupus and Dips

Breads

Index Continued

Desserts

Brownies and Muffins —

Cakes —

Cookies and Bars —

Index Continued

Desserts
Manju, Mochi, Kanten and Yokan —

Pies, Tarts and Flans —

Specialties —

Index Continued

Dressings and Sauces

Entrees

Beef —

Calamari —

Chicken —

Index Continued

Entrees (continued)

Index Continued

Index Continued

Entrees
Scallops —

Shrimp —

Vegetarian —

Index Continued

Salads

Soups

Index Continued

Vegetables

Notes

Notes